PHILOSOPHY

PUSSYCATS

&

PORN

STOYA

ISBN: 978-1-945649-21-9

Edited by Safia Elhillo
Proofread by Rhiannon McGavin
Cover design by Shaun Roberts
Illustrations by Dana Fiona
Editorial design by Ian DeLucca

Not a Cult
Los Angeles, CA

Printed in Canada

Acknowledgements:

"Can We Learn About Privacy From Porn Stars?" and "Can there Be Good Porn" were originally published in the *New York Times* as op-eds on March 8, 2014 and March 4, 2018 respectively.

"Nooooooodie Girl" was originally published in *Coming Out Like a Porn Star: Essays on Pornography, Protection, and Privacy* on October 20, 2015.

"Emma Livry and AB1576" appeared first on *Dazed.com* under the title "Porn performer or prima ballerina? They aren't so different" on December 15, 2014.

"Road-Tripping with Stoya" was first published in the March 2018 edition of *Hustler*.

Index

Icons

January 12, 2018

Theme Warning: Religion, Alienation

Someone said, the other day, that hell is isolation. That hell is disconnection from the universe.

A friend and I went to the Museum of Yugoslavia. As we were walking back to the bus, or trolley—can't remember which—I understood a new layer to a question I'd been thinking about.

I understood another part of my fascination with the Sveti (Saint) icons. They're representations of people—people who had real, complicated lives and have been turned into stories.

I'm far from a saint, but I have a real, complicated life. And I have been turned—numerous times—into a story. Sometimes I participate. Sometimes it happens without my input or permission. It's a side-effect of micro-celebrity.

Note the absence of qualitative judgment.

It is what it is, and I'm not ready to give up on my work yet—neither the porn or the being human in public, not that one doesn't stem from the other. But, sometimes, whatever people dump in my lap won't wash off as easily as I'd like.

People frequently see me as a two-dimensional representation, and twist my timeline to suit the narrative they have in their heads. They project their shame or their need for inspiration onto me. Sometimes with a disconcerting amount of hatred or worship in their eyes. It's dehumanizing. It's part of the job.

When I was a guest on the *Guys We Fucked* podcast, I described this as being on a pedestal in a garbage can.

Women tell me that they absolutely adore [insert fairytale idea of my life or quality so incredibly not me that I wonder if they've got me confused with another performer.] Men bring me their bad behavior or their burning desire to be "good" and ask me to bless their actions, like some kind of whore priest.

This projection and desire for absolution must serve some basic human need, otherwise it wouldn't continue. Otherwise I wouldn't be so frequently objectified this way. We need some force greater than ourselves to hang our hopes and hurts on.

In the West, we've replaced pagan and Greco-Roman pantheon gods with the one-true-God of Abrahamic religions, that God with kings, kings with actors and musicians, and now we've added reality stars and the occasional porn star to the mix.

(I've been told Nietzsche talks about this, but I haven't read much of him. Maybe when I'm done thinking on religion I'll turn back to philosophy.)

We call these entertainers "icons" when they reach a certain level of prowess or fame within their field. I've been called an icon, by members of the press and by people I considered peers until they put me on that pedestal.

When I feel so alienated that I wonder how much longer I can bear it, the saints of the Orthodox Church help me feel less weird and alone in a way that no friend or therapist can.

Sometimes, when I can herd my thoughts into a somewhat linear path, the meaning turns out to have been staring me in the face the whole time.

Graphic Depictions, Scene 01

March 10, 2015

Jiz Lee is everything delightful about sex poured into the body of an often-naked genderqueer hero. Lily LaBeau is one of the most gorgeous creatures to ever share her vulva with the world. They've gazed at each other across the places they perform in for years. Now, here, they are finally coming together. And we get to watch.

Is porn reflecting life or is life reflecting porn?

The answer is both. But if we're defining pornography as portrayals of sexual subjects for the purposes of arousal, we can't neatly parse specific activities or habits into the separate categories of 'sex' and 'pornography'. This is because all partnered sex involves observation of some kind, though not necessarily visual.

Each layer of being observed tends to bring an increase in reaction to that observation, a heightened degree of communication via moans, panting, writhing.

Have you ever masturbated alone at home with the doors locked, window coverings drawn, and lights off? If you have, I'd guess you were much more internally focused than you are when having sex with a partner.

Now add a partner to that pitch-black room. Assuming all five of your senses are functioning typically, you can smell their pheromones, taste any part of them you put your mouth on, hear them mutter unintelligible encouragements or shout commands to keep going, and feel their warmth and sweat.

Take that same partner and turn the lights on: you might become more conscious of the parts of your body on display to them, and appreciative of the visual stimulation their body may provide.

Bring other people into the room: the sexual acts you're engaged in take on a degree of performance, both for the pleasure of your audience and as interaction the two of you might take pleasure in—you might derive enjoyment from giving others a show.

Now imagine yourself in front of a camera and absorb the knowledge that the resulting video will be seen by unknown thousands, hopefully millions, of people: this is what working as a performer in adult videos is like.

The ways in which people have sex in pornographic videos are a natural, authentic response to all those layers of observation.

So what we have here, in this scene between Jiz and Lily, is an ouroboros of looking. They look at each other, and both know that I am looking at them. We are all aware of the crew, the camera, and the collective weight of all the eyeballs that will hopefully view the resulting video.

Also, they're beautiful and covered in rhinestones and having sex with each other. Which is a major part of why we look at pornography, right? To watch people having sex together?

But What is Porn-Porn?

August 2, 2017

Apneatic was in my kitchen the other day. She's a human nude model, not a personification of sleep disorder.

She was describing a shoot she'd done recently, and Steve Prue said he didn't realize she'd started shooting porn-porn (as opposed to soft-porn, art-porn, sort-of-porn.) Both of us turned to him all like "That isn't really porn-porn," prompting him to ask what the demarcation line of porn-porn is.

I shouted, as I do, that it's only really porn when you wake up in the middle of the night worrying about a spelling error on the 2257 age-verification documents. It's only really porn when you dread some kind of cop busting in demanding to see that paperwork.

It's only really porn when VISA gives you a hard time and AmEx won't even touch you. When you don't know when your bank account might be closed, much less have any chance of getting a small business loan.

When you're shut out of PayPal, paying ~13% instead of ~3% for a payment processor. When Big-Cartel will host your store but you can't sell videos because that violates Stripe's TOS.

When you're unsearchable on Patreon/Tumblr/ etc., waiting for Facebook or some armchair hacker to out your legal name—making it easier for strangers to call every aspect of you garbage, instead of just your public persona.

I'd add it's only really porn when doctors routinely insist on an even fresher HIV test than the one you just had done the prior week, but that's specific to on-camera talent.

Clearly, I'm a bit tired of art dudes collecting the street cred of pornography while knowing that they can talk their way out of trouble if they shoot in the streets, while Kickstarting their books, while keeping their mainstream clients.

Even though a lot of those dudes are acquaintances, and some them are close friends and confidants. Their nipples are not a deleting offense on Instagram, and mine are.

It's not about sharing the suffering, so much as sharing the effort to access the same level of infrastructure that media companies broadcasting hardcore violence or hateful misogyny can use.

Dear Supervert

December 30, 2012

I have no recollection of how I found pervscan. com. I do remember being impressed by how legit-imately perverted the content was. It was, at times, highly disturbing. It was always fascinating. When you stopped publishing, on February 14th, I assumed the selection of that date was purposeful. But was it ironic? Hopeful? Done without any deeper motiva-tion than the desire to make people wonder about the significance? Quite possibly it was actually random or coincidental.

There are plenty of deeper, more intellectual-ly challenging layers in your work, but man, is the gross-out factor high at first glance. It's unsettling in a way that forces the provocation of thought. The intri-cacy is mesmerizing. Alien sex hobbyists kidnapping young girls to act out their fantasies on, people having sex with corpses or preying on the emotional turmoil of others at funerals. I've read *Perversity Think Tank* a number of times and I'm positive I still don't truly understand that one. The cover reminds me of Soul-ages. When I first touched it, I pictured slightly hairy hands, protruding from the sleeves of a blue button down shirt and brown tweed blazer, artfully glopping the paint on each jacket. Then I pictured a woman in a men's undershirt, her bare just-got-back-from-vaca-tion-tan ass seated in a leather chair, doing the glop-ping under your direction. Then I wondered whether you were a man or a woman, even though the text of *Perversity Think Tank* indicated you are male.

See, at some point I developed a sustained im-

7

pulse that could be defined as a fanaticism for the true bizarreness of your writing. When I ran out of books and website content, I read other people's thoughts on your work. I found a handful of interviews. The absence of personal information was astonishing. At a time when it seems like nearly everyone puts the details of their life on the Internet and there are people who actually do post pictures of every single meal they consume, you were nearly impossible to find any background on. About two pages away from the end of Google's search results on "Supervert," I started to feel a bit obsessed. It's one matter to consume all of a person's work and do a bit of research. It's another to go to the ends of the Internet and build imaginary caricatures of them in your head. I went ahead and finished reading the last few search results.

What I perceived as your meticulous control of your brand's image became beautiful to me. I began to value your personal anonymity for both its rarity and for the stark frame it provided your work. I developed an additional zeal, solely for this absence of information. Earlier this year I gave a professional acquaintance the cold shoulder for weeks because he emailed me a link to an article which confirmed you are male and mentioned your name.

A few weeks ago, I was setting up my aerial rigging at an event. A woman whose photography was being exhibited at the same event introduced herself (or maybe I introduced myself) and said that she'd seen the "Hysterical Literature" video. She knew you, and told me that you might be attending. I loudly blurted out that I didn't want to know ANY of those details. I then attempted to explain why, and eventually gave up when every sentence felt crazier than the last.

It's chilly where I am sitting right now. 49 degrees, to be precise. I'm wearing a silk robe with panties and men's athletic socks. There are rivulets of sweat sliding down my ribcage from my armpits, just remembering that moment. I do think I might be able to explain it now:

Supervert is an object... a brand... an entity that stands completely independent of the person who created it. You're like the Wizard of Depravity, and what lies behind the curtain could shake my blind devotion or add another exquisite note. I want to revel in my awe of the giant talking head a little bit longer before I look.

Can There Be Good Porn?

March 4, 2018

(Originally published in the New York Times.)

In 2006, when I first considered performing in a hard-core pornographic video, I also thought about what sort of career doors would close once I'd had sex in front of a camera. Being a schoolteacher came to mind, but that was fine, since I didn't want the responsibility of shaping young minds.

And yet thanks to this country's nonfunctional sex education system and the ubiquitous access to porn by anyone with an internet connection, I have that responsibility anyway. Sometimes it keeps me awake at night — but I try to do what I can.

Pornography was not intended as a sex education program. It was not intended to dictate sexual practices, or to be a how-to guide. While some pornographers, like Nina Hartley and Jessica Drake, do create explicitly educational content, pornography is largely an entertainment medium for adults.

But we're in a moment when the industry is once again under scrutiny. Pornography, we're told, is warping the way young people, especially young men, think about sex, in ways that can be dangerous. (The Florida Legislature even implied last month that I and my kind are more worrisome than AR-15s when it voted to declare pornography a public health hazard, even as it declined to consider a ban on sales of assault weapons.)

I'm invested in the creation and spread of good pornography, even though I can't say for certain what that looks like yet. We still don't have a solid definition of what pornography is, much less a consensus on what makes it good or ethical. Nor does putting limits on the ways sexuality and sexual interactions are presented seem like a Pandora's box we want to open: What right do we have to dictate the way adult performers have sex with one another, or what is good and normal, aside from requiring that it be consensual?

Still, some pornographers have been taking steps to try to minimize porn's potential harm to young people and adults for years. And one way we've been trying to do so is by putting our work into its proper context.

Context reminds people of all the things they don't see in the final product. It underscores that pornography is a performance, that just as in ballet or professional wrestling, we are putting on a show. For years the B.D.S.M.-focused website Kink provided context for its sex scenes through a project called Behind Kink, with videos that showed the scenes being planned and performers stating their limits. Their films also showed a practice called "aftercare," in which participants in an intense B.D.S.M. experience discuss what they've just done and how they're feeling about it. (Unfortunately, the Behind Kink project lost momentum and appears to have stalled out in 2016.)

Shine Louise Houston, whose production company is dedicated to queer pornography, has livestreamed behind the scenes from the set, enabling viewers to see what making pornography is really like. I have always tried to provide at least minimum context for my explicit work, through blog posts and in promotional copy.

Many other performers and directors maintain blogs or write articles discussing scenes they particularly enjoyed doing or sets they liked being on, and generally allowing the curious to get a peek behind the metaphorical curtain. Some, like Tyler Knight, Asa Akira, Christy Canyon, Annie Sprinkle and Danny Wylde, have written memoirs.

When viewers have access to context, they can see us discussing our boundaries, talking about getting screened for sexually transmittable infections and chatting about how we choose partners. Occasionally, they can even see us laying bare how we navigate the murky intersection of capitalism, publicity and sexuality.

But this context is usually stripped out when a work is pirated and uploaded to one of the many "free tube" sites that offer material without charge. These sites are where the bulk of pornography is being viewed online, and by definition don't require a credit card — making it easier for minors to see porn. And so the problems that come with porn are inseparable from the way it's distributed.

How it's distributed also shapes the type of porn that is most readily available to teenagers. I frequently hear pornography maligned as catering only to men. That's not quite fair: Most heterosexual pornography caters to one type of man, yes, but to ignore the rest does a disservice the pornographers who have been creating work with a female gaze, or for the female gaze, for decades.

Candida Royalle founded Femme Productions in 1984 and Femme Distribution in 1986. Ovidie and Erika Lust have been making pornography aimed at women for over 10 years. Of course, their work also isn't the sort of content that's easy to find on free sites. But plenty of men enjoy this sort of work, too — just as some women like seeing bleach blondes on their knees.

Sex and sexual fantasies are complicated. So much of emotionally safer sex is dependent on knowing and paying attention to your partner. We in the industry can add context to our work, but I don't know that it's possible, at the end of the day, for what is meant to be an entertainment medium to regularly demonstrate concepts as intangible as these. We cannot rely on pornography to teach empathy, the ability to read body language, or how to discuss sexual boundaries — especially when we're talking about young people who have never had sex. Porn will never be a replacement for sex education.

But porn is also not going anywhere. That means that we have a choice to make. We can hide our heads in the sand, or we can — in addition to pushing for real lessons on sex for young people again — tackle the job of understanding the range of what porn is, evaluating what's working and what we can qualitatively judge as good, and try to build a better industry and cultural understanding of sex. I choose to try.

Fire Escape

November 10, 2014

He was tall. He had a lighter, features striking enough to distract me from his beard. First eye contact was the little zap of a violet wand turned down low, the dynamic pinch of a rubber band snapping on skin. Interest piqued for a second, or four.

Brief, superficial pleasantries were exchanged. Conversation deepened into commiseration over relationships recently ended. "You're so tall," I observed, with an unlit cigarette held close to my mouth. His hand reached out with a lighter. "And you have a lighter."

I'm fantastically un-witty when I'm drunk. I was never great at flirting. Aside from a few people who had been scheduled and compensated, I hadn't had sex with anyone other than my former significant other for two years. I hadn't even been very interested in sex for a few months.

But, that night, I wanted to explore the possibility of being fucked by this man. I turned to the host of the party, and asked if there was any reason not to have sex with this handsome person whose name I hadn't quite retained the pronunciation of. She turned to the friend who'd brought him, repeated the question. A game of promiscuity telephone.

No reason not to, aside from the slowly dawning realization that I'd be having sex at him that night, in his general direction, certainly not with. He seemed too nice, too emotionally honest to be treated that way.

I disappeared back into the center of the party and grasped for some small, stupid excuse to be turned off.

I gave him my email address anyway. I blew off his first attempt at meeting up, but agreed the second time to coffee near a bookstore I needed to go to the next afternoon. I was standing on the sidewalk, leaning against the exterior wall of the coffee shop I'd remembered as less loud than it actually was. Over the top of the book I'd acquired I saw him walk up.

In broad daylight, sober, he was still dashing. His British-accented apology for his slightly late arrival was charming. I was grateful I'd scheduled more coffee with a friend later, and had a hard out in an hour and forty-five minutes. He deserved my full attention, still more than I felt confident in my ability to give. I wished I'd worn clothes that were a little less grubby than my leggings and hoodie.

We sat in a park, then meandered around blocks. He was interesting. He'd canceled a meeting to see me. I was flattered enough for my cheeks to flush slightly. There was a brief hug at the end, the shoulders-and-collarbones-only kind. An attempt to fight attraction with distance.

Another flurry of emails, a date for dinner. The choice of place was left up to me and I managed to pick somewhere with little more than a bare bones bar menu. But it had framed illustrations on the walls and some kind of historical significance that I couldn't remember and we didn't Google.

Later, we got lost (which he also apologized for) trying to find a bar in the West Village. I didn't tell him this, but I didn't care. We could've sat on the curb to talk and I would've been perfectly content. We did eventually find that bar, and you could (as he'd promised) still smoke in it. Our gaze met across the table for a moment too long and I forgot how to breathe. My eyes cut to the side, towards the floor.

"You're so tall. And you have a lighter. And... and I find you very handsome." Another protracted stare with small upturns of the corners of both our mouths, after which I was told that I'm beautiful and intimidating. I didn't feel like much of a superhero at the time, so I made a fumbling attempt to explain how being physically penetrated by parts of another person's body carries a certain intimacy more invasive than the act of penetrating another person, to express that I wasn't sure if I was ready for that even though I wanted it with him.

The time for theory had passed, though, making space for the most awkward cross-table kiss imaginable.

I invited him back to my hotel room, because kissing him for however many hours were left until his flight home seemed like the most enjoyable way to spend that span between night and morning. In the back of a cab, with our legs tangled and my shoulders resting against his chest, I felt his heartbeat and breathed in the scent of him.

Outside the hotel, we smoked one last cigarette before heading upstairs. I'd twined my arm around his. He squeezed my hand and talked about missing being touched so much. I replied that what I missed was that open and fully present touching before all the hurt, walls, distance. That the real, intimate touching sometimes disappears as a warning of the end of a relationship, months before the final parting. His soft "yes" sounded surprised.

Instead of the wiry black hair I expected, I found a blond down on his arms and legs. His skin was softer than a man's should fairly be. Soft enough that I didn't miss my own decadent bed, which I hadn't seen in months. He smelled like warm skin, clean but definitely not sterilized. No overbearingly perfumed soap in the way of his pheromones, which were so very right.

Garments peeled off as the small, writhing movements of heated kissing turned into a mutual rhythm. His mouth found all the best parts of my body to have a mouth on. Both of my legs wrapped around the thick muscles of his right thigh. An orgasm surprised me, and I thanked him for it.

His response of disbelief made me sad. I very much wanted that small scrap of his trust to be mine. A silly intimacy to desire, but wanted nonetheless.

I was thinking then that maybe we'd have sex. He was tugging the strap of my thong towards my knees. I asked what his plans were once he got those off. He'd also been thinking maybe we'd have sex.

By then I had rolled mostly on top of him. The scale of our bodies with the position I was in made me feel small and also powerful—a wiry tyrant in full control. Out loud, I pondered how I felt in that moment about an isolated act of promiscuity. This tall, dark, and handsome war correspondent leaving the next day for the Middle East sounded like exactly the reason one night stands were invented. The pinnacle of romantic glamour.

There was a third apology, this time for struggling with the currently foreign sensation of a condom. He didn't ask to take it off, he didn't whine about responsible use of them, he just apologized with that sweet

British sorry. Sorry for a failure to meet whatever level of sexual prowess he'd decided I must deserve or demand.

My chin rested on his ribcage as I said "We're going to have to discuss this one." And then, "What is sex?" Sex was when two people got together and satisfied each other. "So what is satisfaction?" as I moved lower, cheek between his ribs and hip bone. He chuckled. I sucked all the latex taste off of his cock.

Later, in the wee hours of the morning, he was asleep. His arms unconsciously alternated between gentle enclosure, like a cage built to protect some precious, delicate object, and squeezing me as tightly as possible without crushing. The aftertaste of his semen lingered in the back of my throat, somehow familiar. As I lay there listening to his pleasant snore and trying not to stroke his arm too much,

I recognized the taste.

It was of my favorite scotch. The peaty one I describe as tasting like good testicles in the summer, masculine and complex. The difficult-to-find one with the exotic backstory. The one I'll walk just about any number of blocks in impractical shoes to find. The analogy was too much to process, aside from fleeting thoughts of "so fucked" and "why now, here." So I went to sleep, too. And then he was gone.

Window

November 24, 2014

The New York Soho House, whatever it was initially built for, feels like a playground for those with too much money and too little sense. This is how I justified sneaking through its corridors with a very attractive man, searching for a dark corner to touch each other in. Not to imply that either of us possess too much money, or that he possesses too little sense.

New York City is full of people, piled on top of each other and squished into multi-story buildings. You have to love people, or love grumbling about them, to exist happily here. There's a public quality to daily life, more so than in a city built on people transporting themselves in private vehicles.

So many concepts around sex are grey, including the general boundaries of what intensity of interaction is appropriate in which settings. Because I'm conscious of the discomfort that can be inspired in others by overt displays of sexuality in public, I try to be conscious of the effects of those displays. Try in no way means that I succeed—I'm comparatively oblivious and also very myopic when aroused by a wonderful person.

Because of my career, I'm also wary. I'm not egotistical enough to believe that every move I make is of interest to someone likely to record it on searchable parts of the Internet. But I also know that once a proximity or attachment is on public record, it can be used to discredit people who have become associated with me, and I prefer to avoid casually inflicting that on others.

Buy the ticket, ride the ride, yes. But I feel a responsibility to explain the details and potential ramifications of the ride before that ticket is indelibly obtained.

All of that said, Soho House feels secretive and permissive. As though any behavior, up to the point where they throw you out, is acceptable. A place where premium is paid in exchange for permitting any impulse.

I live on the south end of Brooklyn and he lives somewhere in Queens. This seems convenient, both places being in New York City, until you bring bus schedules and traffic into it. Because it is two trains and at least one bus, probably more. Our evenings out in Manhattan all end with me writhing around, pouting that he won't come home with me, and trying to decipher why, specifically, he keeps saying I'm trouble.

So we snuck and explored, through the winding halls and up and down staircases. There were no dark corners. Not in the movie theater, not in the library we couldn't actually find, and certainly not in the brightly lit sitting area next to a storage room. And the storage room turned out to include a staircase which looked highly trafficked.

The brightly lit sitting area did have a large window, though. Sheer curtains against the glass blocked the view across rooftops, towards the Hudson River. The sill was just wide enough for me to kneel on, and thick curtains hung on the outside of it.

I sat on that sill and tugged at the curtains. He asked how we were going to make this work, and I said I didn't know but we would. He climbed in after me, and then we did make it work, in a desperate and cramped way, until he pushed his cock as far into my mouth as it could possibly go and came down my throat.

I swallowed and giggled as I pulled those sheer curtains aside and looked out across my city, because every detail in that moment was good.

Can We Learn About Privacy From Porn Stars?

March 8, 2014

(Originally published in The New York Times.)

I didn't expect to become a porn star. People rarely do. I was 19 years old, and my photographer roommate had an offer from a website to buy some nude pictures. We did a shoot and then waited two weeks in case I woke up in a panic over the idea of releasing naked photos of myself into the world. But I didn't, and so I turned to the required paperwork. One of the boxes to fill in read "Stage Name (if applicable)."

Stage names are common in the entertainment industry — whether in Hollywood, rap or pornography — and they're used for all sorts of reasons. But at a time when people can be whoever they like on the Internet, when we are all negotiating who we are in which setting and for which audience, somehow the combination of a woman whose job is fantasy and her fantasy professional name can make people lose their minds.

Consider the recent hysteria over the Duke University student who moonlights as an adult film starlet. Although it didn't take long after the news broke for her fellow students and strangers to gleefully post her legal name online, "the Duke porn star," as she has been called by media outlets from *Forbes* to *The Guardian*, has tried to control what she is called where. She used the pseudonym Lauren when giving interviews, and the pseudonym Aurora for her stage name in those same interviews. Finally, this week, she acknowledged her actual stage name — Belle Knox.

The whole kerfuffle doesn't need to be as dramatic as people seem to think. For me, choosing a stage name felt less like concealing my identity (especially since I'd just turned over my Social Security number to strangers) and more like deciding on a user name for any Internet service or website.

I chose Stoya because it was there. It was a diminutive of my grandmother's maiden name, and my mother had considered it before naming me after Jessica Savitch, the news anchor. Spoken aloud, Stoya had a nice balance between femininity and strength. It felt rightfully mine because of the family history. An insurance agent owned the domain stoya.com, but I didn't think I'd ever need a website of my own.

I wasn't a voluptuous sex symbol or exotic glamazon. How big could the market be for pasty young women with wacky sartorial tastes and wiry limbs? I expected my orifices to be viewable in high definition by anyone with an Internet connection. I did not expect to have a career as a performer in hard-core videos, much less to see photos of myself on magazine covers or to be regularly recognized on the street. It would be ragingly narcissistic to assume that over 150,000 people would follow you on Twitter because of your work in pornography. But eight years later, that's exactly what has happened.

Not everyone performing in adult films uses a stage name. Tera Patrick has said she legally changed her name to match her professional one. A few use their whole legal name; others keep their given name while taking a suggestive or unique surname. Still more take Love or Star, sometimes with creative spellings, and I'd support a 10-year ban on every iteration of both.

Along with desires to differentiate themselves from performers in similar fields, increase ease of spelling and pronunciation or convey a certain image, some performers do take a stage name for the purpose of making themselves more difficult to recognize. This might possibly have worked in the '70s, but with easy access to enormous amounts of adult content on the Internet and the ease with which we can all find juicy tidbits of information about one another's pasts online, I can't see it having much effect anymore.

I am on the board of the Adult Performer Advocacy Committee, which offers peer-to-peer education and supports performers' rights. In the introduction to its Porn 101 video, my colleagues explain: "There is a great likelihood that everyone you know will see these images, or at least find out," and "You cannot expect your legal name to remain a secret, and a stage name will not fool people who recognize you."

My stage name is less about withholding parts of myself or maintaining privacy than it is a symbol of the idea that I am more than just my job or any other isolated slice of my identity.

The strangers who call me Jessica at publicity appearances lean in far too close. They hiss it as if they have top-secret information. All they're doing is letting me know that they had 30 seconds to spend on Google and no sense of propriety — which may sound funny coming from a woman who flagrantly disregards it herself. They're often the same people who refer to my orifices as "that" instead of "your," as though the body part in question is running around free-range instead of attached to a person with free will and autonomy.

Yes, there's a paradox here in that I willingly engage in work that reduces me to a few sexual facets of myself but expect to be seen as a multifaceted person outside of that work. I participate in an illusion of easy physical access, and sometimes the products associated with that illusion — the video clips and silicone replicas of my sexual organs (seriously, and they're popular enough to provide the bulk of my income) — do, in fact, exist without attachment to a person with free will or autonomy.

But this same lack of context is a situation any of us can experience. It's what happens when any ill-advised tweet or embarrassing Facebook picture goes viral. Ten years ago, I would have judged people over the course of several conversations. Now I evaluate them based on a few snippets of their social media presence. Whether you portray yourself as a professional sex symbol or a morally upstanding member of the PTA, we all do this kind of self-branding now.

Maybe it would be easier to navigate the dissolving boundaries between public and private spaces if we all had a variety of names with which to signal the aspects of ourselves currently on display. And maybe we should remember that our first glimpse of a person is just one small piece of who they really are.

Economics

December 8, 2014

The little muscles under my jaw felt like they were being shredded from the inside. My eyes leaked. The salt burned my face, and I wondered if my tears were causing the abraded feeling in my throat.

My emotional meltdowns tend to be spectacularly melty. This one was no exception. Somewhere between tear three and tear six, I became a scene. As in "causing a scene."

Except I wasn't causing a scene, I just was a scene; a bipedal black hole of emotional distress. If I'd been a theatrical show I would've involved excessive pyro, three different sets of confetti cannons, and fifty-seven synchronized chorus girls with rhinestone headdresses.

Since I was not a theatrical show, I just cried into my coffee on a sidewalk in downtown Los Angeles. I slid down the wall into a crouch and clutched the edge of my rolling suitcase. My awareness of my spectacle did not help me contain myself.

A resident of Skid Row was slowly pushing a shopping cart full of bedding and tin cans down that same sidewalk. He had metallic blue cat ears perched on his head. He asked if I could spare a cigarette. I could, and did. As I handed it to him, he made eye contact.

He thanked me, lit the cigarette, and informed me that I looked like I was having a bad day.

I nodded; he was correct.

He then asked why I was so sad. As I prepared to articulate the gist of my emotional pain, those indi-

27

vidual tears turned to streams. My face crumpled and I sobbed at his sympathy.

I only stopped sobbing when he asked if I'd like some of his heroin.

I can't handle that high so I don't ingest it, just like I don't ingest rum, or extremely spicy foods, or any other substance my body reacts to negatively. But when I said no, I said no, *thank you*.

Because I was grateful. Because if I was evaluating acts of kindness on percentage of resources offered, it might be the nicest gift anyone has ever tried to give me.

Nooooooooodie Girl

October 20, 2015

Murphy's Law of Inappropriate Behavior states that if you make a habit of taking your clothes off in public, eventually everyone in your family (including members so distant they share less DNA with you than a chimpanzee does with a cuttlefish) will somehow stumble upon documentation of what you're up to.

My grandmother is a very smart woman, and I'd been dodging the question of what I did for a living for at least three professionally naked years. I really had been meaning to tell her about my job before she found out from the television or a newspaper, but I thought I'd do it when I was ready. "Ready" consistently being defined as any time except for right now.

So I was completely unprepared when she called and said, "Your mother says that you're sort of like a model. I don't know what that means because if you were a model she would just say you're a model, and you're a bit short for that anyway. No offense, dear. What do you do with your days?"

I wished I'd discussed this inevitability with my mom or had some legitimate reason to get off the phone. My usually dodgy cell service was clear as a bell.

I worried: What if I failed at easing her into the whole idea of my career in pornography and she had a heart attack, leaving me accidentally guilty of grand-matricide? What if she decided to just cut me out of her life?

More pressing—how was I supposed to explain

what a modern pornographic actress was to a woman who doesn't know how to work a cell phone and still had typesetting tools laying around from her days in advertising?

"Well, um, do you remember Bettie Page and pin-up? What I do is kind of like pinup but more explicit. Like, with no clothes on."

"Oh! So you're a noooooooodie girl!" Either I was hallucinating or that statement had been delivered in a positive tone.

"Yes, ma'am. But, uh, pop culture is a bit more edgy now than things were in the '50s, so I have actual sex with people and it goes on video or DVD."

"In the mooooving pic-tures! Do you enjoy it?"

"I have fun. It's always interesting. I only do things that I want to do, with people that I want to do them with. It's good."

"Well then, that's all very nice and I'm glad to hear you're doing something you like."

Since the conversation was going so well, I figured we might as well get everything over with at once.

"There's something else I should probably tell you while we're on this subject."

"Ohhh?"

In addition to being smart, my grandmother is an incredibly expressive woman. You know that Mehrabian's rule thing about how communication is 93 percent nonverbal? In my grandma's case, 99 percent of communication is pure vocal inflection. There's something in the way she draws out the vowels. They become a whole adventure.

This particular "ohhh" had started out some distance into curiosity land, passed over the gosh-what-else-could-top-the-last-thingmountains, and settled on the patiently-waiting-to-hear-more plains.

"I'm using your name as my stage name. Well, I'm using the Americanized diminutive. The point is, I'm using part of your name as my stage name."

"Vera? That's not very sexy."

"No, ma'am. I mean, I think Vera could actually be quite marketable with the current neoburlesque scene, but I'm using Stoya."

"Oh? Oh."

The first oh was surprised, and the second oh sounded less than enthused. In my head, I stared into the largest imaginable pit of uh-oh. I wondered if she could hear my heart pounding over the phone. My left hand frantically picked at the stitches on the hem of my shirt. I became concerned that I might be the one to have the heart attack, and I wasn't going to die without one last cigarette. I lit up, inhaled and exhaled, inhaled and exhaled again. Finally, I couldn't take the extended silence any longer.

"Gramma?"

"I was just thinking. I hope none of the men at the nursing home get us confused and try to put my feet behind my head. I don't bend that way anymore." Apparently, since the death of her last husband, she'd acquired three boyfriends. Because it takes that many of them to keep up with her. My stressful and dramatic coming-out-to-Grandma moment turned into a farce because although the promiscuity gene may have skipped a generation, it most definitely runs in my family.

Bruise

November 20, 2014

Very little in life is as simple as it looks through the constraints of headlines, tweets, and text messages. There are always multiple perspectives from which a given situation can be seen. A certain level of opacity seems right when discussing events which involve parts of other people's lives that they typically prefer to keep private, and the parts people typically keep private are what I live in.

That said, I was in a romantic and sexual relationship with another person for approximately two and half years. That relationship ended. I believe it needed to end and that I needed it to end. This belief has no effect on the fact that I hurt in ways I can't currently understand.

Fifty-four days after I left that relationship, my body reminded me that I was in pain. I was constantly cold, my urine was nearly as dark as the scotch I'd been ingesting, and my heart felt both shredded and compressed. Please understand that none of this information is a request for any attempt at medical diagnosis. I am merely relaying the contextual whys behind getting in the shower and taking internal stock of my body.

Once I was out and mostly dry I looked at my skin:

There's a brown bruise on the side of my neck, thumb-sized but left by a mouth. A series of green spots trickling down my left arm and a mauve one under my right breast. Dark red marks from teeth and fingernails streak the left edge of my torso. Most of

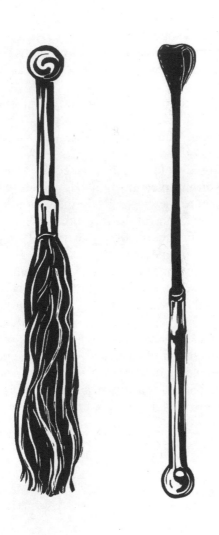

my left thigh is pink and lavender.

I've worn the marks of broken capillaries as symbols of deep games of physical ownership and power dynamic. I've displayed them to indicate sexual tastes, and sometimes to flaunt those tastes in the face of that straw creature named normative, vanilla, basic. Because sometimes I am a gleefully indecent muckraker.

I've wanted them for the physical sensations during the process of being bruised. I've loved the look of them. The bones and the whipcord muscles and the marks.

The night before, I had asked for these bruises, said yes and please. My hands pulled the person giving them to me closer. I said thank you because I wanted them. None of the pleasurepain spectrum activities we engaged in were unexplored for me, but my thoughts around them were.

These particular marks, they're a reminder that wounds and scrapes do heal. I can randomly guess but not accurately forecast how long it will take. Physical and visible manifestations will shift through various stages before they are actually better. The sensations and presentations of pain will change a number of times before they disappear.

I poked one of the bruises and thought about how typical my grasp for pseudo-control really was.

Sigh

November 17, 2014

When I spoke at Barnard last week, someone asked me how I approach being recognized in public. I said that I don't approach it. It approaches me.

Usually, people who strike up a conversation in public because they know my work are incredibly nice and very respectful. More likely than a friendly hello is a tweet or email from someone saying they think they saw me but didn't want to interrupt my book, phone conversation, coffee.

A couple of months ago, I was sitting in the window of a coffee shop near Washington Square Park, reading Houellebecq's 'Platform.' I'd taken a dislike to it on page sixteen but was determined to read through to the end before making a final judgment. From close behind my right shoulder, I heard a sharp, tense "Hi!"

I turned to see a man standing over me. He was talking fast, saying "It's me, you know me, I say hi to you all the time, you know me." His right hand extended, waiting to be shaken.

I didn't think I knew him, but I do meet an extraordinary amount of people every year and am sometimes slow to recognize them.

I stared blankly as his recitation of "you know me, I say hi to you all the time" continued. When he added "It's me, the writer" I did know him and also knew I wanted him to go away.

In early 2011, he'd approached me at a train station. He'd excitedly informed me that he'd seen a video of me just the night before and had written this script he'd like me to read. He had at least one copy in his bag, and pressed it into my hands.

I can't remember if I gave him my email address to make him go away or if he dug it up on the Internet. Either way, I received an email later saying he'd meant to ask me for my real name. I replied that I didn't appreciate questions from strangers about my legal name.

Undeterred by lack of further response from me, his emails continued: asking what city I was in, expressing sadness we hadn't become pen pals, saying Happy Memorial Day. Easily archived like other unwanted communications and harmless compared to many other statements and sentiments people send via the Internet.

Back at the coffee shop, his hand still hung expectantly in midair.

I was full of no. No, I don't want to talk to you, I want you to leave me alone. No, I will not shake your hand, I want you to leave me alone. No, I will not look anywhere other than my book because you aren't taking a verbal no for an answer and so I will not engage in any more discussion.

Eventually he retracted his hand and left.

I relaxed and actually read the page I'd been staring at. I refused to be pushed out of the comfortable chair I'd chosen in that coffee shop until I was ready to leave. If we're going to have an entitlement-off, some presumably male person's perceived right to my attention vs. my right to exist outside of my apartment unharassed in a city I think of as my home, my entitlement will win.

Twenty minutes later he came back, threw himself down in the seat next to mine, and exclaimed that he needed me to understand because he needed me to be his friend, needed me to like him. The stakes felt higher now and I felt scared. I gathered my belongings, abandoned my coffee, and backed towards the counter where employees were preparing to close up for the night.

When I reached the back of the shop I asked if I could just hang out with them for a few moments. They looked towards the entrance and said they'd seen that guy before, that they thought he was kind of creepy. I filled them in briefly on the backstory.

He was gone, but one employee told me to stay back there for a moment and poked their head out the front door. They came back and reported that he was lurking a few doors down, asked if they should call the police.

I was shaking by then, fight or flight response in high gear. I did some fear-based weighing of my options: The police as a general category are not my friends. Between my time spent in Philadelphia and New York City I've personally witnessed enough abuse of power by those in uniform to be wary by default. I've seen plenty of documentation of far worse abuse in the forms of institutionalized racism and excessive force.

But how was I going to get from this closing coffee shop to my next destination without risking being followed by this man? And, more concerning in the long term, what if I eventually ran into him a third time? What if that interaction wasn't harmless? What if I then needed to file a report and was asked why I hadn't done so this time?

So we called the cops. As soon as the vehicle pulled up with its red and blue flashing lights the man ran off. I recounted the whole interaction to the two officers, they filled out their paperwork, and then they walked outside with me to wait while I hailed a cab.

As I opened the car door, one of the officers said he was having drinks with friends the next night and was wondering if I'd want to come along. I told him I didn't think that would be appropriate, climbed in, and shut the door.

A friend expressed sympathy via text, reminded me of the ways we can protect ourselves, and tweeted frustration about the incident while maintaining my privacy. My tangled ball of feelings sat inside me for a couple of weeks, until I called the precinct to get the report number.

Once I was on the phone I felt like I had to bring up that officer's behavior. When they asked which officer it had been and I gave their name, they responded with a resigned sigh. A sigh that sounded like this wasn't surprising.

I thought, my god, these cops...they really do all seem like bastards.

KGB

December 1, 2014

I had a meeting that afternoon. The coffee was very good. I drank too much of it. By the time I walked the handful of blocks to KGB Bar, I was shaky. My bones and skin felt cold. My muscles and tendons and blood burned in comparison. I'd say I was feverish, but I'd prefer to avoid gothic romance novel territory.

When I got upstairs and poked my head into the bar, I didn't recognize anyone. The closest seat to the door was open, so I sat in it and looked ceilingward. Shiny tin showed through chips in the matte black paint. The canopy of the closest light fixture dangled askew. The room glowed red.

Friends started to trickle in. They found me staring up with wide eyes and a tense mouth. I was nervous. One asked how I could be. I'd already been asking myself that same question.

There's this frantic tension I get before any performance. If it were diagrammed it would be an asymmetrical cartoon starburst. Self-doubt is in there for sure. A bit of impostor syndrome branching off of the doubt. Some healthy fear—an ingrained habit from live aerial shows where overconfident sloppiness could lead to severe injury. Aerial acrobatics is the only work I've ever done that required me to sign liability waivers and have my own special insurance.

I believe that tangled, spiky mess means you still give a shit.

I do love this panicked feeling. Maybe in the way I imagine people who love rollercoasters enjoy that moment before the terrifying drop. I can't say for sure because I don't like roller coasters at all. If I'm going to freak out my sympathetic nervous system I prefer to do so with real stakes: my metaphorical heart, career, actual physical wellbeing.

On to the part where I directly contradict myself:

Most work involving cameras has the safety net of editing. You have multiple takes or a series of still photos to choose from afterwards . Any awful or awkward moments can be left to die on a hard drive. The stakes are lower because of this net, but then higher again because whatever doesn't die on that drive is public record for as long as the Internet exists in any form resembling its current one.

With live performance there are no second takes, but also less documentation (unless someone is hiding a cell phone in their jacket and stealthily recording). I've been performing for live audiences long enough to have built up a series of quirks and routines that serve as a coping crutch before live shows.

Reading a personal essay in a room full of strangers though… I'd never done it before and didn't have a single appropriate trick up my sleeve to calm myself. Having never done it meant I didn't know how to productively direct my panic.

And the room did fill, becoming what a person who goes by FuckTheory on Twitter later described as "a steam room on whiskey." They were definitely not wrong.

As the temperature rose, sweat trickled down the sides of my ribcage. I began to regret wearing the visually interesting yet super itchy polyester dress I'd chosen for the evening. I wanted it off. Partial nudity is one of those inappropriate coping mechanisms I referred to earlier.

I said to the semi-circle of friends that I was very nervous and I might go stress masturbate in the bathroom. Two of them offered to help. KGB has some of the most public women's toilet stalls I've ever seen, and the porn star being chucked out of the Adult Magazine reading early because of public finger-fuckery was just too predictable of a role to inhabit.

Instead they pressed various types of whiskey (bourbon, scotch, rye) into my hand for sipping and squeezed their own hands against my one non-drinking hand supportively. (Hands, hands, so many hands.) A cuddle puddle started to form in the doorway to the room. I drew comfort from it.

Eventually, my name was called to read. I shuffled my way past the standing audience, then through those sitting on the floor near the podium. Safely hidden behind this glorified soapbox, I slipped off my shoes.

I'd written the piece barefoot and somewhat terrified of the judgement that comes from public disclosure of emotion. Over the past few months, I'd started rocking back and forth while writing and editing, like a human metronome. In private, this tick works and isn't widely seen, so it evades judgement. In public, I'm afraid it will look crazy.

I wouldn't allow my body to move while reading in the way that it moved while writing, but at least I could be barefoot and terrified. Definitely terrified, to an unusually high-pitched degree. I remember the escalating squeak in my voice, the overly bright reading light, and Sarah Nicole Prickett's beautiful face when she interjected "Oh, that guy!"

When she interjected I thought I might be off the hook. Maybe I'd gone on for too long and she was verbally giving me the vaudevillian shepherd's crook? No such luck, though, even after my enthusiastic "yes, that guy" and an excruciatingly awkward pause. So I continued through to the open-ended end.

After the end-end, I found my purse and escaped into the night air. When I exhaled that breath it took most of my tension with it. Not necessarily better, but a more interesting release than that unprivate toilet could have accommodated.

Acting

November 21, 2017

I've always had a twitch about the term "porn actor." The phrase never felt accurate when applied to my work. Sure, some of the on-camera talent in pornography thinks of what they do as acting, but I don't. I think of my day job as performing.

Yes, many of the scenes I've done during my career contain what we refer to as "set-up" or dialogue. This precursor to sex is usually treated as secondary, and the more vocal consumers often express derision for it. The shooting conditions rarely allow for more than a handful of takes per angle. There's no rehearsal.

The actual sex scenes are easiest to do all in one take. Every pause or stop reduces the energy. They're more like a feat of athletic prowess. The bulk of the story—a very simple one that focuses on physical sexuality—is told with the body, not the voice. This makes performing in porn more like dancing to me than acting.

So then why am I talking about acting? I've done some.

———

A couple of years ago, I went to Serbia to make a movie. (Lazar Bodroza and Dimitrije Vojnov's *Ederlezi Rising*, releasing 2018). I'd agreed to do the project based on a five-page treatment. It sounded like a challenge, and I like Serbia.

Securing the funding took years. There were rehearsals and coaching and screen tests before the actual shoot, and the actor I'd initially worked with was replaced.

Just before we began principal photography, we had another week of rehearsals. We tried each scene multiple ways, with different sets of blocking. I had to learn a few simple martial arts moves, and how to safely perform them, so we drilled that all week as well.

We shot an average of two scenes per day. When we thought we'd gotten the shot, everyone would gather around the monitor to watch it. One time, I noticed that my hand was contradicting both my statements and the rest of my body language, so we re-did the scene.

Workdays were almost exactly twelve hours. There was a single instance of overtime at the request of both the lead actor and I, and we were only granted one more take, so only a few minutes. Everything was precise.

———

From late October to late November 2017, I was in a play. (Ian W. Hill and Dean Haspiel's *Harakiri Kane or Die! Die, Again!!*) It started with a reading in Phil Cruise's living room so Dean could hear the play out loud. Then Phil asked if I'd participate in a public reading. Apparently, these events are useful for feedback.

Later, around the time Ian decided to direct the show, they asked if I'd be interested in doing theater. It sounded like a challenge, and by this point I liked the people who were involved.

I read with potential lead actors during casting. We did another private reading and rehearsed. About a week and a half before the show opened, we did a run-through as a group. That was when I realized I was about to be in a play, in New York City, with a bunch of experienced and well-trained people. I started to get nervous.

See, there's no doing it over or checking your script in live theater. There's no "let me try it a different way since the timing didn't quite land on that one." There's no "oops, when do I talk?" You have to remember your lines, blocking, which emotions change at what points, and—the most difficult for me—to project your voice.

A few minutes before the house opened for the first show, I started to feel the physical symptoms of nervousness—the dizziness, pounding heart, sweat. They stopped when the show started. Weirdly, they came back about 15 minutes after I got home. Like the adrenaline of showtime had given me a pause but not a reprieve.

I started to relax about halfway through the ten-show run. The last show, of course, is where I did my best work.

———

It turns out, there's a commonality with all three types of work (pornography, video acting, and stage acting) of being in the present moment, in the little bubble contained by the viewer or lens. If they can't see it, it doesn't exist.

I was surprised by the differences between video and stage acting. Stage is much more difficult, but the sense of accomplishment is stronger and occurs after every show. There's a stronger connection to the audience and there's immediate feedback. Both can be very fun with the right people.

If you've been following me for a while, you know I don't tend towards flowery speeches of gratitude. I am grateful to every person who came to see the show. A full house that is engaged with what they're seeing makes the experience of performing that much better. An audience that participates—gasps, cringes, laughs—is the best reward.

Thank you.

Guest Informant, Warren Ellis

March 26, 2012

During my years as an adult performer, I've spent more time talking to press and interacting with people on the internet than I've spent actually having sex. It was, for me, one of the unexpected parts of being a contract star. Most of the porn industry interviews are pretty standard. They want to know what our favorite positions are, how long we've been in the business, what turns us on, and who we'd like to work with next.

The interactions with the mainstream press are where it gets interesting. Radio personalities, reporters from newspapers and magazines sold without plastic shielding their covers – they ask more complicated questions. They want to know why we have sex on camera for a living. They want to know how our parents feel, what we think about the effect of our jobs on society's view of women, whether we believe we're setting feminism back or moving it forward (the answer is neither). They want to discuss the issues people get worked up about. They want to talk about condoms vs. testing, the idea that porn molds sexual behavior in a way that reaches beyond the consumers of it and the people they have sex with.

All I ever have for them is an opinion. Usually my opinion is a bit different than the opinion of someone who hasn't spent time with sex workers. After this opinion has been given the reporter wants to discuss it. Debate it. Play a metaphorical volleyball game where this opinion is tossed back and forth until one side is convinced that the other is speaking truth.

I had to fake knowledge of volleyball during the filming of a XXX remake of Top Gun last year. I wasn't so convincing with the sports, but when it comes to debating the case for a healthy place for porn in sexuality I've had a pretty decent success rate.

Perception equals truth. Before the 18th century, people knew that everything revolved around the Earth. Galileo couldn't argue convincingly enough against the Catholic Church and if you stand outside without the benefit of what we consider basic scientific education, it really does look like our planet is the center of everything. One viewpoint might be scientifically wrong, but both beliefs are true to the people who believe them. Galileo went down historically as right because he doggedly presented evidence that corroborated his beliefs on heliocentrism until the day he died.

Sometimes people quote things I said at the beginning of my career and I wonder what I could possibly have been thinking. In retrospect I think some of the statements I've made were oversimplified or just incorrect, based on bad information and faulty logic. Somewhere out there are people who started out disagreeing with me and ended up agreeing. It doesn't seem like it matters whether I'm right or wrong. What matters is how convincingly I can defend my position.

In politics, there is actually a campaign tactic referred to as the 'charm offensive.' It's not about whether you're right or wrong, it's about how charming, personable, and stubborn you can be when someone sticks a microphone in your face.

Which brings me to something resembling a point: question… vocally. Question the things I say, question your newspapers, television reporters and favorite blog. Question the things you thought and the things you think now. It's the only way any of us are going to grow…

…or maybe I'm wrong.

Patriarchy!

December 22, 2014

I was in Queens, shortly after 3 am. The temperature was below thirty-two degrees Fahrenheit and I was wrapped in a long list of garments: a hat, three shirts of increasing size, topped by a hooded sweatshirt and coat, a thick scarf covering the lower half of my face, with a pair of insulating long underwear under a pair of pants, boots, and gloves. The only visible parts of my body were my eyes and the bridge of my nose.

A man walked past, leering, and spoke at me in Italian. Mumble, mumble, bella.

My most intense interaction with the Italian language occurred on an adult film set while Rocco Siffredi and I engaged in a significant percentage of the possible appendage/orifice combinations we could achieve with our bodies. Towards the end of this scene, I forgot to let the camera get a shot of his ejaculate congealing in my mouth before swallowing it. But I still managed to pick up enough of the language to know when I'm being spoken to in a sexually explicit manner.

My assumption of catcalling by this strange man in Queens was confirmed by the *ch-mueee-ch-mueee* sound of those classic kiss-y noises emanating from his mouth. Any man attempting to employ that sound as a pickup tactic should know that even my actual-feline cats respond to it with disdain.

When we were four feet past each other, I'd heard enough of his tooth-sucking come-ons. I turned to face him. My lip was curled and I was about to raise my arm to point at him while shouting "Patriarchy!" This has become my way of noticing, of reminding myself that "normal" does not equal acceptable.

Then, I heard the person I was meeting say "Hey."

I thought about how it was actually freezing. I thought about the potential ramifications of a shouting match on a corner covered in cop cars. And so I turned back around and I let it slide.

Later, the person I had been in Queens to see made a comment that indicated they thought of street harassment as potentially linked to revealing dresses.

Hellfire and Socialist Sex

September 10, 2017

There's a burlesque troupe in NYC called Wasabassco. They do an extra-risque monthly show called the Hellfire Club and I was able to catch it last weekend.

There's a compelling, joyful quality to boldly gyrating women. Like, okay, the news is terrifying, but Nasty Canasta's comedic timing is spot-on. Yeah, we might actually be headed to hell in a handbasket but Sydni Devereaux's beautiful face is still beautiful and she makes the most engaging expressions with it on stage.

Hope in hilarious hedonism, as it were.

———

In preparation for the first Sex Lit event, I read through Bataille's *Erotism*. I think the context of his philosophy is important to understanding his earlier pornographic work.

In chapter eleven, Bataille says "There are people who turn up their noses at these statistics, but, for all their imperfections, can they not see how valuable a Soviet Kinsey Report would be?"

I found it difficult to imagine that there wasn't one. So I emailed a friend of mine who writes about politics and people, and pays attention to sexuality.

My friend turned up a work called *General Sexual Pathology* from the mid-seventies. He also mentioned that there is a Serbian word for multiple men lined up to have sexual intercourse with a woman.

———

I've always been curious about gang bangs. Why

we call them gang bangs instead of fuck puddles or cock buffets. Why the bangee is so frequently shown in a position of submission, with the bangers standing over them.

So what is this Serbian word, and how aggressive are the connotations of it? Do the political systems of a population change the dynamics of group sex? Maybe I need to return to the Balkans.

Emma Livry and AB1576

December 15, 2014

(Reprinted from "State of Sex" in *Dazed*)

I went to Bluestockings in Manhattan recently and left with a stack of books. One of the books was Deirdre Kelly's *Ballerina: Sex, Scandal, and Suffering Behind the Symbol of Perfection*. It starts out exactly as salaciously as the title implies, and ends with a discussion of modern steps towards better workers' rights and healthier job conditions. Somewhere in the middle is a relatively extensive retelling of Emma Livry's story.

I was prepubescent and enrolled in a significant number of ballet classes when I first heard of Emma Livry. She was so fantastically talented that the great Marie Taglioni herself was moved to choreograph *Le papillon* for Livry to dance the starring role in. After performing the role of Farfalla the Butterfly, whose wings are burnt as a catalyst for the happy ending, Livry herself was burnt during a rehearsal for *The Mute Girl of Portici*. Her costume was set alight by the open flames of stage lighting. And she died, because it was the mid-nineteenth century and antibiotics hadn't been invented yet – which is definitely an ending, but difficult to classify as a happy one.

I'm unsure about the intentions of the instructor who told me this anecdote. It could have been an attempt to instill gratitude for modern medical science or a desire to impart knowledge of a notable moment in the history of dance.

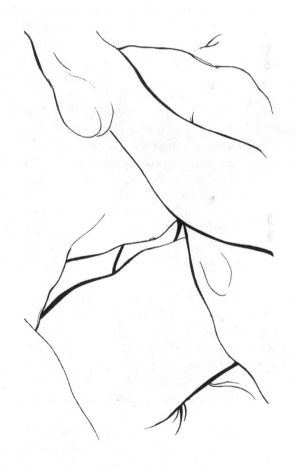

My initial takeaway was that Emma Livry, the last major dancer of the Romantic Era, died in the most Romantic, with a capital R, way imaginable.

(Don't act like Byron and his peers weren't the poster children for opulent morbidity.)

I had no idea, until midway through reading Kelly's *Ballerina*, that the French government had introduced legislation, years before Livry's accident, which required costumes to be treated with flame retardant chemicals. I also had no idea that a number of dancers had refused to wear the treated tutus because the chemicals made their skirts dingy and stiff, spoiling the ethereal effect they went through years of punishing physical training to achieve.

Livry, despite having witnessed the narrowly averted death by burning of one of her coworkers, was one of the dancers who wrote letters to the Paris Opera protesting the flame resistant costumes. "I insist, sir, on dancing all first performances of the ballet in my ordinary ballet skirt, and I take it upon myself all responsibility for anything that may occur," she wrote .

After being set on fire by a stage light, experiencing burns on more than a third of her body, and suffering through treatments in which lemon juice was squeezed into her wounds, someone asked Livry if her opinions on flame retardant chemicals had changed. She acknowledged the increased safety, but maintained that she still would not wear them if she were ever able to return to work.

Dancing in a stage production, like performing in an adult film, feels like a combination of practicing the craft of performance and acting to fulfill the director's vision. The likely risks of dancing include chronic snap-crackle-popping of joints at a young age, maybe a fractured or broken bone here and there. The likely risks of performing in adult entertainment include ostracization by family, peers, or society at large, and difficulty securing other employment later in life.

Both careers tend to have an upper age limit, typically under thirty-five. Risks are taken and sacrifices are made for a chance at success. That success a slim possibility, and even if it is achieved, it lasts for a very short window of time.

To enter either profession is to accept the likelihood of certain harmful side effects and the risk of more serious damage. The sacrifices I've made for my work were willing, but they were sacrifices nonetheless. I would appreciate the freedom to continue evaluating which risks I feel are worth taking, which safety measures I deem most helpful in each situation.

While I was reading *Ballerina*, I was spending most of my work hours attempting to hunt down a currently working adult performer who was pro-AB1576 and willing to give me an interview regarding why. California's AB1576 bill is the latest in a string of county and state legislation geared towards forcing adult performers to use condoms in sex scenes as a prophylactic, in spite of virtual mountains of statements from performers saying that what they want is the ability to choose for themselves which safety measures to use. I never did find a performer who agrees with AB1576, much less one willing to discuss it on public record.

I was struck by the similarities between the responses of the Paris Opera dancers and the reactions of California-based adult performers to outside legislation. I thought that I should probably be reacting to these new pieces of Emma Livry's story by taking them as a warning – but I wasn't reacting that way, and my opinion on forced barrier use at work didn't change. I just admired Emma's dedication to her work.

I'm definitely not arguing for a dedicated pornography wing in the Louvre, but I would absolutely argue that adult videos are a kind of art. They are, after all, generally protected in the United States under the First Amendment. Pornography has undeniable mass appeal, and speaks to one of the most basic human needs. While it frequently caters to the lowest common denominator in an effort to be financially viable, it does occasionally produce timeless works. Consider Bettie Page, who appeared in pictures which were classified as pornographic at the time and are now deemed suitable for travel mugs and refrigerator magnets.

Like Emma Livry's distaste for stiff skirts spoiling her illusion of weightlessness, I dislike the idea of being forced to use barrier protection when the accompanying friction impedes my ability to deliver the best performance possible. If members of the French government had listened to the dancers they were trying to protect, they could have explored options like moving the lights two feet forward or enclosing them in cages. Maybe the real lesson here is that performers and artists will do their work in the ways they consider best, and harm reduction can only be effective when their requirements are considered first.

Paris

January 23, 2015

The director met me over eggs before the wardrobe fitting. He was wearing a suit made from the deepest navy blue velvet and managing to make it work. He was possibly aided by the fact that any warm material seemed reasonable to wear in these temperatures.

One of the producers walked me around afterwards. I peeked over a bridge that crossed the Seine. Verified that the Pompidou Center still looks like a water treatment plant flipped inside-out. Saw a single building, encrusted with green art nouveau vegetation, that was so beautiful I wanted to stare at it forever.

Another producer drove me past la Republique's monument, currently covered in signs declaring Je Suis and Nous Sommes Charlie. While there's no way to compare two tragedies, nor am I encouraging any attempt to do so, I wondered what our country would be like if it were the sort of place where the Statue of Liberty was draped in banners of solidarity with Eric Garner.

The first producer came back and took me to dinner. A grey tabby climbed over the tables and shelves as she pleased, eventually curling up on my lap. When the food arrived, I gave her little shreds of meat and scratched her under the chin while she purred.

That morning, I leaned out of a window to smoke. A pair of lavender striped panties hung off a sill across the courtyard, under a nubbly wall covered in dirt I suspected was as old as I am.

Paris: the surprise extra installment

January 30, 2015

I got to see Jessa, an old friend from Philadelphia who I hadn't spoken with since 2009. We'd lost touch during one of my stints living in LA. She'd moved to Europe shortly after. We exchanged a flurry of emails before I arrived, and arranged to meet at a cafe. Squeals, hugs, and catching up all ensued. She's a beautiful tattooist now, by which I mean she is still beautiful and also does beautiful work.

Mature women peeked out of the doorways in the neighborhood I stayed in, wearing lace lingerie with contrasting embroidery, stockings, and covered by dark fur coats. They wore large brimmed hats and red, red lips. I was told that they were street-based sex workers. Many had a spare, genuine smile for me.

On what was supposed to be my last morning, a handsome man brought me pastries and espresso in bed. I'd wanted to run my fingers through his hair for (hyperbolic) ages, had discussed with my old friend the difficulty I was having discerning whether he was flirting or just French.

He was flirting.

He was also fantastic to kiss with, starting with soft pressing of lips to lips, taking the time to find my rhythm and meet me halfway. When he moved his mouth to my neck and his fingers to my cunt I came and came and came, or maybe I just didn't stop coming. Either way it was wonderful. Then, with his fingers inside me and his mouth between my legs, I had the most cliched small death of an orgasm I've ever experienced.

When I pulled his pants down I found I unwrinkled testicles and a gorgeously proportioned cock. My tongue left a trail of saliva on his shaft, which I wrapped my hand around and stroked until his semen hit the back of my throat.

Paris is delicious.

A woman on the metro spoke against racism to an audience held captive between stops. My minuscule grasp of the language turned her words into a song of justified, controlled anger.

My flight was cancelled because of the snowstorm. I was on forced vacation then, with a dead laptop battery, no charger, and spotty Internet access on my phone. But who among the gluten-tolerant can really consider themselves *stuck* in France?

I woke up menstruating and hurried through the streets looking for a pharmacy.

Jessa tattooed me; "Negative Impact on Public Health," quoted from the 9th circuit's decision to uphold Measure B. The catalyst for both my politics and my writing, under my skin.

I think it's important to remember—how I felt reading that ruling, that to parts of the world I and all sex workers will always be reduced to inhuman vectors of disease and societal ill.

The tattoo pinched a bit, only really registering as painful towards the center of my chest. The sun-burnt feeling in the hours afterwards hurt more. Then I gave her a little pixel-cat on her lower leg.

On what would turn out to actually be my last morning, I walked through Pigalle. There's a solitude I love about red-light districts before they open for business, different from what I love about them at night.

An impromptu visit to the Dorcel office was interrupted by a call saying I needed to get to the airport for a flight that had suddenly become available.

Back at the apartment, I threw my belongings into my bag. The handsome man came back to say goodbye while I waited for the taxi. As soon as he was across the threshold of the apartment his arms were around me and his tongue was in my mouth. I kicked the door shut without breaking the kiss.

There's that cinematic cliche again.

We threw ourselves onto the bed. With one hand on each of my ass-cheeks he ground my pelvis into his until I came, screaming into his ear. I bemoaned the blood. No time to deal with clean-up meant there was no time to fuck.

I made it through border control and security just in time to eat lunch before boarding.

Slow Correspondence

January 3, 2015

I'd taken this white tunic (Balenciaga, F/W 2012, on mega sale at Bergdorf's for $40) and transcribed the first few chapters of Bataille's "Story of the Eye" onto it with black fine point Sharpie. I did this because I wanted it to exist in the world so I could wear it to the Adult Entertainment Expo that year. After the expo, it stank like Vegas; stale smoke, sickly remnants of other women's fig oil and suburban mall brand Freesia body spray, the nervous sweat of a thousand overstimulated porn consumers.

So I threw the tunic in the washing machine on a delicate-cold/cold setting. When it came out showing heavy signs of ink bleed I thought that while visible decay was fitting for such a garment, it should die not through sanitation but through accrual of physical stain.

I wore it regularly for the better part of two years. Sun faded the writing on the shoulders and my own nervous sweat progressively yellowed the arm holes. Streaks of dirt collected on the hem. I knew it was a matter of time before I perioded* all over the shirt, because that's what happens to white textiles around people with irregular menstrual cycles.

(*Yes, I just used the word *perioded*. A past tense verb, to be precise. This is my book and I'll perpetuate abuse of the English language if I want to.)

This fall, a friend presented me with a bound paper object, limited edition already and made even more unique by the destructive personalization enacted on its pages over an evening of cocktails. This gift

was the most invaluable in a string of gifts they'd given to the world, to me indirectly and directly.

After I'd read the pristine copy of their newest book and stowed it safely next to the desecrated one, I felt sad that I had no appropriate response. I remembered a line of theirs about the acid body of a woman staining a gown. I had an impulse that felt crazed but precisely right. It had to be done.

The tunic went into an envelope. The envelope went to them. Weeks passed with no response and I wondered if it'd been lost or if I'd crossed a line. Then I received an email with an audio file. I sent a text to Clayton Cubitt saying shit had just gotten weird and Clayton reminded me that my relationship with this person(a) has been very weird for quite some time.

Two months later the mp3 remains unheard. Its mere existence and the possibilities it contains still give me such a thrill that the idea of listening to it feels overwhelming, like I'd melt or fly apart or both.

Blood, sweat, and ink indeed. Long live the filth.

Blow

June 7, 2016

Philadelphia, under a table, at a nightclub. Both of us were dedicated sluts, and during work was just so much dirtier than going home together after.

Burbank, California, in the driver's seat of a parked car. I had, for the first and possibly only time, a desire to 69.

Delaware, someone's basement, a couch. It seemed like, and was, more entertaining than spending another evening playing pool.

Brooklyn, NYC, a bed. It was his birthday. My lingerie had bows on it. I'd planned it that way.

Matsue, Japan, a modified cargo container. I had far too much Shochu in my system, an early train in the morning, and we couldn't manage to trigger my gag reflex any other way.

Virginia, an Amtrak train, the bathroom. It was so close to Erica Jong's zipless fuck, how could I not?

Paris, France, his office, 2 am. He'd taken me there on the back of his moped. I blew him on the couch—his desk chair might've been too cliche of a location.

Red Hook, Brooklyn, NYC, I thought my mouth on his dick would make a nice addition to the finger I had up his butt. It did.

Rittenhouse, Philadelphia, an alley. We had a low but existing chance of being caught. Managed risk gives me goosebumps.

West Village, NYC, a sublet. Last day of May. I knew, from the previous time, that the liquid glossing over the tip of his cock tasted so good it could turn addicting.

Belgrade, Serbia, a bed. Even though I was writing his check that day, all I wanted to do was suck Mickey off like it was my job.

Dicks

January 16, 2015

A few weeks ago I said "There's really no nice way to explain to a person that you just don't care that much about the size of their penis, or its turgidity." This seemed to be largely understood as a comment on unsolicited dick pics, but I just mute or block the people who send those. On Twitter, on my phone--if I don't have a way to shut down unwanted communication, I tend to avoid the technology itself.

What I was referring to was the shy or reluctant penis. The penis attached to a person who thinks they must provide a brick of an erection at the slightest hint of a partner's sexual desire. Attached to those who apologize profusely for what they interpret as an insult to my physical allure, what they fear is a failure to meet basic requirements.

I encounter the bearers of these complicated cocks fairly regularly in the wild. The part I struggle with is how to gently communicate the fact that, in a recreational setting, I really don't care.

A hard cock is not the key to pleasant or fulfilling sexual interaction. I don't have any cocks at all and manage to make myself feel quite good whenever I have the desire. Having a lower orifice penetrated by a cock raises the various risks of sex. A condom might break and cause a flurry of unscheduled STI testing and a trip to the pharmacy for Plan B. Even if the condom stays intact, the next-day itch from vigorous abrasion by latex is one of my least favorite sensations.

When these male-bodied people begin to stress, I say, "It is totally okay. If your penis decides to present itself as a viable option for vaginal penetration, that might be fun, but there's a whole range of other stuff we could be doing." They say, "Thank you for being so nice," while believing precisely zero of my statement and stressing doubly. They get stuck in their heads about it. Their manhood becomes threatened by their own adherence to a paint-by-numbers conception of heterosex.

But in my bed, the person with the semi- or wholly flaccid organ is the only one focused on the absence of its tumescence. And I've never found a nice way to state my lack of concern in a way that will be believed.

Until recently, a man would respond exuberantly to my mouth and hands, but shrink as he suggested penetration of my vagina. His deep purple glands disappearing into his foreskin expressed disagreement with his words. He would begin to apologize, excuse, but then would ask if he could go down on me.

With my back arched and both shaking legs wrapped around his neck. With two of his fingers firmly stroking (but not stabbing) the front wall of my vagina. His tongue gently stroking my clit. That's how "See, who needs dicks?" gets its point across effectively.

Tease

February 14, 2015

I'm not releasing any new videos yet, so I know I'm just being a tease by talking about shooting explicit videos.

But I, at least partially, like being a tease.

There's also something I like about booking shoots. I like telling the director of photography what energy and aesthetic I'm after, adore working out scheduling to get the talent I want. It makes me feel like a boss.

A *fucking* boss.

Last week, I carefully shuffled through the slushy streets of New York, occasionally jabbing the heel of my boot into an unavoidable patch of ice. I was on the way to a photoshoot for an unspecified fashion magazine. Everyone on the team (except the makeup artist) was a young woman in college.

They had a shot list. For a magazine editorial. I was blown away by the level of organization and professionalism they were operating at.

When the day was over, I walked up to the Village. Frozen rain hit me in the face, and I thought, if these kids are any indication of our future then the future is gloriously bright.

Neither of the projects I just discussed have a release date.

There's a time warp that happens with production of media. Work is being shot but release dates depend on the schedules of editors, publications, and—in the case of my explicit videos—billing processor approval.

Conversations about work frequently go like this:

"What've you been up to?"

"[insert project here]"

"When does that come out?"

"That depends on when ____ and ____ happen."

"When is ____ going to happen?"

"Good question. I have no reasonably accurate answer."

Squicks and Squees

July 21, 2015

A long damn time ago, like 362 whole days, Fiona Duncan asked if she could interview me about language as it relates to porn.

The semantics of sex are interesting to me, and Fiona looked cute on Twitter, and then we were on the phone. During our call, she expressed a desire for a negative search option when browsing porn: "like, "school girl" plus "pubic hair" plus "threesome" minus "hard boob job" minus "dude gut.""

And that got me thinking, about how people still like to browse garment stores even though they can search up exactly what they're looking for online: "blue chambray" plus "short sleeves" plus "loose fit" minus "$100+.""

The next time I saw Kayden, she mentioned the way that every experience is novel to a child, how, as we live, our greater knowledge of the world means there are fewer novel experiences to come across, and how that tends to make novelty feel more valuable.

So: a number of people are accessing porn by typing long, specific search strings into a browser—helping them find what they want but immensely narrowing the field of new variations they might discover. Some people value surprises they enjoy. People also have specific details or acts they would prefer to avoid, but these are multitudinous and highly individual.

People have their squicks, and they also have their squees. At some point during the design of TRENCHCOATx 1.0 (as the site appeared after mid-June 2015. Before mid-June was TRENCHCOATx beta and I don't even want to talk about it) I asked our new web designer if they could make a customizable negative search profile for our customers, and our designer said yes.

So I sat in my apartment for days on end, tagging every video we have with every specific I could think of off the top of my head: analingus, armpit hair, ejaculation: on face, vulva, penis, uncircumcised and circumcised, three levels of pubic grooming, and breasts: augmented or natural.

The list continues for quite a while, but can't begin to reach comprehensive without some major feedback from consumers. It will probably never be complete.

As of today, we're (super) proud to introduce a pair of new features on TRENCHCOATX.com: Squick Protection and Squee Enhancement. Any logged-in user can choose both specifics that squick them out and details that make them squee from a list of tags, have their squicks either completely hidden from them as long as they're logged in, or be warned if a video they're considering contains one or more of their squicks, and have videos that contain their squees highlighted.

Fun, right?

We don't go so far as to call it a trigger warning feature, because while some triggers may be obvious others are sometimes indecipherable. There's no way to guarantee no viewer will never be triggered during a scene that they're watching. But this does enable people to create a safer space to explore adult content.

And I'm so very excited to keep digging into the semantics of sex.

As of 31 December 2016 Stoya is no longer involved with TRENCHCOATx. com. She wishes them the best and has no idea whether Squicks and Squees are still in use.

Tubes vs. Torrents: the Ethics of Piracy

March 4, 2015

While the cost to produce a work and the need to recoup that cost in order to make further production feasible—much less a viable career—does bear mentioning, more interesting to me are the ethics of piracy.

The adult film industry has been in a downward spiral of budget slashing for years. Performers' rates have remained generally unchanged while inflation increases each year. Long-term crew members have found themselves replaced by inexperienced people willing to do their jobs for lower pay. The quality of videos made under these conditions tends to suffer.

It is easy to point at online piracy as the reason for the declining sales that are causing these budget cuts, but the situation isn't quite that simple.

A long time ago, when the Internet was much more like the Wild West and adult video companies made their money selling VHS tapes to brick-and-mortar stores, everybody charged too much for their product. Rather, they charged what the upper limit of what the market would bear, knowing the consumer didn't have many options.

As access to the Internet became more widespread, studios popped up to serve the new digital market. This prompted established production companies to either build their own commercial web presences, or sell the rights to their back catalogue for pennies. Shady business practices abounded, including hidden add-ons—inconspicuous pre-checked buttons signing the purchaser up for extra services at extra cost unless actively un-checked, similarly to Columbia House's negative option billing system—and alleged double-processing of credit cards. In his book, *Beaver Street*, Robert Rosen provides rare documentation of a scam involving *High Society* magazine, in which users were asked to verify their age via credit card information to access an ostensibly free tour and then auto-billed $60 a month.

Not that business practices ranging from disingenuous to fraudulent are unique to pornography. Ponzi schemes have existed since the early 1920s, and product subscriptions like Enzyte and Proactiv can be notoriously difficult to cancel. But dirt is always dirtier when it's in porn's backyard.

By the mid-2000s, when free tube sites full of explicit streaming videos arrived on the scene, the online porn viewing audience was primed to adore them. They'd been overcharged; they'd been taught that giving their credit card information to an adult site could result in theft. It is difficult to blame them for choosing to watch stolen and freely distributed content, given the risk involved with paying for it.

According to a 2011 feature in *New York*, a man named Fabian Thylmann bought a company named Mansef in 2010, to mash their tube sites and other properties together to form a new company called Manwin.

Take a minute to look at that name: Manwin. Man. Win. The name seems to drip patriarchal entitlement.

Manwin's tube sites enabled users to upload whatever they pleased, including videos owned by other production companies. All this free porn helped Manwin grow the traffic flowing to their websites.

As you may already know, when consumers view content on free sites (whether blogs, news outlets, or porn tubes) they're paying with clicks. While that doesn't cost the consumer— other than time and the small amount of energy to engage their finger— it enables the website they're clicking on to generate money.

Manwin used their traffic to sell ad space to those same production companies they enabled theft from. Production companies paid a lot for banners. Manwin then began buying the companies they had helped de-value, including Digital Playground—the company I was contracted to for a number of years. I believe the worst sorts of capitalists would consider Manwin's behavior a win of the highest order.

I see a major difference in intent between torrents and tube sites. With regards to pornography, tubes and torrents are diametrically opposed reactions to the infinite reproducibility of online content.

Torrent sites like the Pirate Bay seem committed to freedom of information and freedom of speech, hosting anonymous leaks exposing government and corporate misconduct alongside copywritten entertainment media. One founder, Peter Sunde, has been incredibly vocal about the overreach of proposed laws like SOPA and PIPA.

Aside from notable exceptions like WoodRocket and PornTube, most of the major tube sites are owned by Manwin (now called MindGeek.) The Manwin/MindGeek network of tubes looks like effective, market crushing monopoly and many of their properties have engaged in "settle or we'll sue" tactics—directly targeting individual downloaders with lawsuits demanding inflated payment for product viewed—

known as copyright trolling.

Would you care to guess which one I'd prefer you pirate my work from? As I start to release the first pornographic videos I've directed (and funded) into the world, I'm wishing the Creative Commons had an Attribution-NonCommercial-ShareAlike-No-TubesOnlyTorrents license. In lieu of that, I have this essay.

So I'd love it if enough people paid for *Graphic Depictions* to make it possible for me to make more work like it, but I don't believe in copyright trolling or cracking down on sharing. Create all the GIFs, clips, and screen grabs you want (just know that the rights to the music belong to Sxip Shirey) and share them with the world, but please don't charge people for them, and please keep the name of the project attached. And please, for the love of all that is filthy and explicit, keep it off the damn Manwin/MindGeek owned tube sites.

Surviving the Spraytanpocalypse, Part 1

February 1, 2017

For over a decade, it has been part of my job to interact with the Internet-at-large. For ten years I read all of my mail. I didn't necessarily respond to it, but I read every Myspace message, then every email and @ on Twitter. I thought it was fair to give a stranger's armchair diagnosis of debilitating dissociation the same amount of consideration I gave to criticism on language use from a member of my wider community. I believed that if I put words and thought out there, it was only right to hear out the responses. And, fuck, did that ever fuck me up.

Reading messages that were sent maliciously—to hurt—isn't the same as being stuck in the same physical space with someone as they scream the words at you, but it's on the same spectrum. Eventually, all those little comments pile up, especially when they're coming in every day. Especially when they're mixed in with important messages you need to see in order to maintain your work and have the money to pay your rent, to help organize protests, or to keep up contact with friends and loved ones.

Eventually, this pile started to get to me. Eventually, a nasty tweet from some random human on the other side of the globe—who was almost certainly never going to act on their threat—was able to poke at the scabs from threats of immediate concern or from my past. Eventually, I found myself going into fight or flight mode every time I opened my computer or unlocked my cell phone.

People tried to help. "Haters gonna hate" was

pulled out of storage and dusted off. Encouragements to ignore [blank] or to not think about [other blank] were given out like Halloween candy in a middle-class US suburb. Eventually, my response was an extremely frustrated "I'D LOVE TO, BUT HOW."

Because, you know, that "don't think about pink elephants" phenomenon.

I tried imagining unresolvable concerns as clouds floating away, and picturing them as leaves falling into a stream before being carried off by the current. Then I bemoaned how ineffective this was for me to a partner, who told me that they handle thoughts they don't need to think about right now with a direct, internal "I don't need to think about this right now.' I was all "OKAY, THANKS, BUT THEN IT STILL COMES BACK."

(It was a very all-caps period of my life, stuck between "Yes, yes, I need to take care of myself" and how the actual fuck to do that.)

To which they replied, "yes, and the trick is to accept that subjects you don't need to think about will pop back into your head, and then calmly address them again with 'I don't need to think about this right now." Once I stopped getting frustrated with my inability to put a thought out of my head permanently, it became slightly easier—and far less emotionally draining—to put those thoughts out of my head until some action could actually be taken regarding them.

Finally, a friend introduced me to Rebecca West's *Black Lamb and Grey Falcon*. It is not light reading and many grains of salt must be taken with it, but somewhere in those 1,200 or so pages was the most effective answer I've found so far to BUT HOW: instead of subtracting bad things, add good things.

Or: When bad things cannot be subtracted, protect the good things and focus on them when you need a break from the bad.

(An individual's good things to think about/focus on will vary, as will what we each have access to. Here are some of mine: cats + laser dot, floating in hot water—which has a 50/50 chance of helping or exacerbating, fucking, sewing silly little decorative bits for friends out of remnants from larger projects.)

The ability to wrangle our brains into actually taking a break from stressors feels important because, without rest—if we are constantly embroiled in skirmish after skirmish—it seems that much harder to find the stamina to win a war.

Friend Love

September 14, 2017

I'm so happy F was there to meddle. I wanted to reach out earlier this year, but I could see from the Internet that you were busy with hugely important political work. I was afraid of introducing turmoil into your life when you seemed already swamped.

When F came up and asked if I'd like to talk to you I said what I've been saying for months: "If she would like to talk to me."

I didn't want to make a scene in the middle of Molly's birthday party. I watched from across the apartment while he asked if you were willing to come to me in the kitchen.

As soon as I saw you nod your head in assent, my face crumpled up in that ugly-happy way that photographs terribly because it's so genuine.

It felt like the conclusion to a Lifetime drama about estranged friends. I suppose that's a sign of how epically I've missed you.

A wise science fiction writer once said something along the lines of real being what doesn't disappear when you stop looking at it. I was pleasantly surprised to find you hadn't disappeared. That we haven't disappeared.

I know you did the best you could last year. Intellectually I've always known that, it just took a very long time for the rest of me to get there. I floated home and can barely wait to catch up properly.

Love, I hug you, I kiss you. I'm so happy to have you in my life again.

Road-Tripping with Stoya

March 1, 2018

(Originally published in Hustler.)

Photographer Steve Prue and I have a professional relationship that has yielded many spreads for brand-name girlie mags, a number of photosets for nude websites, and a plethora of behind the scenes shots. We even published a book (called *Stoya x Team Rockstar*) together.

We've also been roommates for the better part of six years. When I briefly flirted with a return to Los Angeles and promptly noped back home to NYC's public transit and concrete towers, Steve drove the moving truck containing my belongings, my cats, and myself across the country.

I grew up in the southern United States, and road trips were very much a part of that life. In the south it was no big deal to hop in the car for a visit to a historical landmark three states over, or to visit family.

Those of us who live in the coastal cities tend to forget that there's a whole other America. When we reside in, for instance, Los Angeles or New York, we sometimes begin to refer to the rest of the country as "fly-over," or we cease to refer to it at all.

In the wake of last year's Presidential election we've all been reminded of just how much political, religious, and ideological diversity exists in our country. With all the rhetoric about making America great again, I've become nostalgic for the things that symbolize the, well, chiller and more relaxed America. And what's more American than roadside tourist attractions and full-frontal nudity?

So I present, like a postcard from the pre-Trump era, the saga of our great cross-country road adventure:

———

We're leaving California to enter Arizona. Signs by the highway declare "The Grand Canyon State Welcomes You." We decide to skip the obvious entendre of a split in the earth with water running through it and head towards Tombstone instead. Breakfast is at IHOP, where the brown tables are vaguely sticky with half-dried syrup residue.

Once we're on State Route 80 we pass what looks like a film set—huge lights, a trailer set in the dust a few yards away from the highway. I wonder whether it's a documentary or an independent film.

Tombstone's O.K. Corral, thanks to Hollywood magic, is thought of as the site of a legendary gunfight between the Earps, Doc Holliday, and some outlaws who called themselves the Cowboys. This is quite literally the stuff westerns are made of—1957's *Gunfight at the O.K. Corral* ushered the incident into public consciousness.

The altercation actually happened a few buildings away from the corral itself, but *Gunfight in an Empty Lot on Fremont Street* doesn't really have the same ring to it.

I throw some mascara on using the side-view mirror and climb out onto the sidewalk. In front of the historical landmark sign, I pull my shirt up to flash my breasts. We don't have time to wait for the re-enactments, and while the thrill of flashing in public was titillating I'm in a hurry to get out of there before someone catches us. To get back on Interstate 10 we have to backtrack.

As we're approaching those lights again I realize three things: This is a checkpoint, not a movie set, near the Mexican border, we're in a moving truck, and the glove compartment contains a well-intentioned gift of marijuana from California. I chuck the pot out the window as we're rolling to a stop and frantically light up a cigarette to cover the smell.

The officer wants to know where we're from, where we're headed, and how we know each other. This gets complicated rather quickly, and the more I try to explain the more his eyes glaze over. The more he disengages, the more I linger over details.

Pretty quickly he tells us to go ahead with an air of exhaustion. Steve tells me I'm the Unicorn Princess of Too Much Information and encourages me to look into a career in smuggling. I quip back "Working in porn and running away with the sideshow that one time isn't edgy enough?"

The cats are staging a noise demo.

––––––––

The side of the road is intermittently dotted with stands selling turquoise jewelry. We drive past signs welcoming us to "The Land of Enchantment." The landscape is lovely, vast stretches of desert surround huge rocks reaching into the sky. And I suppose both alien abduction and belief in alien abduction could be considered forms of enchantment.

Roswell, New Mexico is close to the site of an unidentified flying object crash in the 40s which fuels conspiracy theories and attracts alien enthusiasts to this day. Many of the local businesses cater to tourists interested in extraterrestrial life, science fiction, and kitsch.

To reach Roswell we have to drive through winding mountain roads. The scenery changes to surprisingly green foliage. As night falls it starts to rain. Then it starts to rain a lot.

We're hoping to find a giant flying saucer—not the one occupied by McDonald's—in the morning to take good butt shots in front of. The weather is awful though, and after zagging down a few of Roswell's massively wide streets we give up on an epic outdoor setting and google up a list of the indoor attractions.

Eventually we settle for some more flashing in the International UFO Museum's library—the one area of the building without CCTV cameras. Since I can't climb into the exhibits and it feels unsanitary to rub their books all over my naked skin, I pretend to steal a dossier titled "Abduction Details." The resulting tableaux is vaguely self-referential, which elicits a giggle from Steve.

We stop at Denny's for dinner, and the staff is utterly checked out. They're barely visible and seem confused by the process of seating people, of handing them menus. We have a delightful time pretending they're all aliens who have been dropped on earth to report back on mundane subjects like how humans feed ourselves. We imagine them reporting back on the ratio of waffles served to waffles eaten, dutifully tallying every sugary soda refill sucked dry by a customer.

The cats have gone full black-bloc, hurling their whole bodies at their cage and knocking over their water.

———

Now that the rain has stopped again I can feel the leather of my shorts sticking to my ass cheeks. My sneaker-clad feet are propped on the dashboard.

Sweat beads up on my skin, rolling down my hamstrings from the backs of my knees.

I start to get restless. I've been folded up in the passenger seat for days now. We pull over at a rest stop so I can run around and climb on the picnic tables. It feels nice to stretch out in the sun for a bit. The hot wind dries me off. Steve pulls his skateboard out and rides around before insisting I pose in front of a fence.

As we enter Texas, the state reminds us to drive safely. I support this sentiment wholeheartedly. The narrow two-lane highways are a bit of a squeeze, and something about the distance of the horizon makes spatial geometry deform.

The rain picks up again and we're slogging through two-foot high floods alongside trucks that are much larger than ours. I can hear the water splashing against the cabin door as we roll by. I become a human proximity alarm, emitting a high-pitched squeal every time we're passed by a big rig.

We eat at Waffle House. I take the opportunity to pull the storage drives and photo/video equipment out of the back of the truck and stash them under my feet on the passenger side of the cabin. Fortunately nothing was damaged.

The cats have gone limp. They attempt to have a sit-in under the bed in the hotel, passively resisting with all their might when I scoop them back into the carrier.

————

We think about stopping by Austin to say hi to the Fleshlight staff. Then we realize the ranch we're staying at is almost totally in the opposite direction and the detour would add a few hours of driving. Some friends of Steve's offered to put us up for the night and let us shoot a whole spread's worth of photos on their property, which was far enough from the road to give plenty of privacy.

We grab some beer before we enter the dry county to leave as a hosts' gift. Steve has classical manners that way.

Dry counties are something I'd forgotten about. When I lived in North Carolina we had the ABC stores. They kept shorter hours than most other sorts of stores did. Where we were coming from, Los Angeles, they sold hard liquor at the grocery stores.

The ranch is cozy. I sat in a rocking chair on the front porch with the lights off, taking in the giant night sky dusted with stars far brighter than they appear from a crowded city. The only thing more humbling, to me, is the infinite variety of sexual acts that can occur between even two people.

There's none of that here, but there's a pleasant recollection of a dashing (seriously, dashing) war journalist I'd fallen in mad crush with the prior week. Freshly connected to wifi, I see I've received an email from them. Fireflies bob and blink across the lawn. The chair gently moves back and forth.

The cats snuggle with me on the bed that night. I think they may have forgiven me.

————

I take a long shower. I wash my hair with plenty of suds, lather and shave my legs. The home's bathroom feels less sterile than the string of hotels had. The coffee is delicious. When my hair is dry, which doesn't take long in the baking Texas sun, we head over to the moving truck to shoot some less arty, more directly pornographic stills.

I climb in the driver's seat for the first time. I'm already sweating from the sun pouring in through the windshield. I'm happy I didn't bother with foundation or much other makeup—most of it was buried deep in the back of the truck.

· The posing is, by this point in my career, second nature. Steve and I have worked together so frequently that we slide into a rhythm, him prompting me to move to the next pose once we've got the exact right shot—the face, body, light, and frame all as they should be at once.

I slide my shirt over my head to reveal the strappy bra underneath, pausing with it wrapped around my wrists. My jeans, which are frankly hideous, slide easily off my hips and pool around my ankles.

(What do you wear on moving day?)

I turn my back towards the camera and reach around to unhook the back of my bra, gazing into the lens. My panties—dotted net in the front—have a sketch of a couple 69ing on the rear. It isn't my favorite position to do, but I think it looks beautiful. I pull the crotch aside to show my pussy.

I step out of the truck and lean against the bumper. The sun-heated metal feels warm against my ass, almost burning. When we've shot enough photos we head out to Louisiana, which, of course, has welcome signs in French.

———

We eat at Cracker Barrel. I stare at the walls stuffed with Things to Decorate With, and understand the success of Michael's. The triangular peg-board game doesn't exactly entertain, but it keeps my fingers busy until the food arrives.

The street slopes in front of the hotel in New Orleans. Someone has to hold the luggage cart steady while I load the cats onto it. There's a bird in the lobby. It's somehow ornate and trendy-feeling at the same time.

A former suicide girl and a friend from the internet of mine stop by the hotel's bar for a drink. We chat about the different kinds of sex work—and saucy work—we've done. Steve tells old stories and snaps an instax mini.

I'm developing a massive head cold from that journalist I'd been kissing before the trip. I have whiskey, and hope it has some kind of medicinal effect. I don't think to go to a drugstore and get Nyquil.

In the morning, Steve skateboards to get beignets. We talk about how we should try to take pictures and decide Bourbon Street with beads is too obvious and that cemeteries are just rude.

The cats have gone on hunger strike. Apparently their recent affection had been one last plea for mercy.

———

We proceed right through Mississippi (claiming itself as the "Birthplace of America's Music," though previous signs stated "It's Like Coming Home"), Alabama (which welcomes visitors to "Sweet Home Alabama") and Georgia (which is glad to be on your mind.) The closer we get to South Carolina, the more frequently the South of the Border signs appear.

South of the Border is a spectacularly racist theme park just over the state line between North and South Carolina. I feel a bit uncomfortable about including it, but I feel deep discomfort over the idea of ignoring it.

We've been so gonzo journalism-style about the trip that to gloss over one of our country's tackiest moments of cultural obliviousness felt wrong. It's a very real part of our nation, just like our rugged founders and our salacious pornographers.

Another real part of our nation is our love for fireworks. South Carolina does a brisk business in them at their border. I refuse to hold sparklers. I want to leave. Steve and I compromise, with me climbing a couple of the donkey statues and him grabbing a couple of quick shots. It is, of course, pouring rain.

I also refuse to sleep at South of the Border. Instead we stay at the motel barely inside North Carolina. The front desk asks for a deposit for the television remote. I lock the cats in the bathroom, not wanting their paws to touch the carpet, and sleep fully clothed—hoodie up—on top of the bedspread.

The cats remain firm in their hunger strike. I begin to feel concerned for their health.

———

There's one last meal at Hardee's before we head home to healthier fare. This is probably for the best, but the grease from that breakfast biscuit is like a warm blanket on the inside of my stomach.

We were planning to spend a night in Virginia but we're close enough to make the rest of the drive today. I'm excited to get home. I'm excited just to head north on I-95. 295, 495, 695, another 295 all scroll past. The further we get up the eastern seaboard, the more traffic there is.

We stop at a Wendy's for lunch. I think about how I should really eat a vegetable or twelve. We drive past many places I'm sure George Washington slept in once, but nothing on the roadside is retro enough to warrant a stop.

The Verrazano-Narrows bridge connecting Staten Island to Brooklyn is very narrow. I start emitting that high-pitched squeal again and don't stop until we're back on land. This begins to irritate Steve.

Eventually we arrive in Brooklyn, where a pair of muscular movers empty the truck and haul everything upstairs. They matched. I wondered, if I pretended to have misplaced my wallet, whether it would play out like a porno.

The cats have not once resulted to violence. I remain unscratched.

Mitcz

February 27, 2015

Almost a decade ago, another lifetime entirely.

When we met, he asked if I was old enough to drink. I responded by sucking a mouthful of well whiskey through the tiny straw, spitting it in his face, and then licking it off.

I wasn't old enough to drink.

We both kept the same late-night hours. I'd just moved to Southern California for the first time, drifting without my social group. He'd pick me up in his car and we'd drive all over Hollywood and the Valley in the middle of the night, talking about absolutely every subject that came to mind. I bluntly flirted and got the slightest hint of interest in return: much discussion about the impropriety he'd exhibit if he were to become physical with me.

One night we drove all the way to San Diego. I think I'd said something about still being unsure the Pacific Ocean actually existed. Why he took me that far to stick my feet in it, I don't know. But he did, and I waded in as the sun came up. It smelled very different from the Atlantic and was much colder.

We got coffee after, and he insisted on paying. In the car, on the way back to LA, I insisted on blowing him. Finally, one of us had checkmated the other.

A week later, we stopped the car in what looked like an empty field, or whatever barren space of sand and dirt served for an empty field in Burbank. I crawled over him, into the drivers' seat. Flipped my body upside down, firmly clasped my legs around his neck to press my cunt into his face, and swallowed as much of his cock as I could.

When we were done I dismounted. Rolled back to the passenger side. And spotted a cyclist.

We'd parked smack in the middle of a bike track and dawn had come while we were distracted. A veritable marathon of 30+ people were cycling around the car. He hurriedly zipped up while I giggled maniacally.

We ran, metaphorically. But we were safely ensconced in the vehicle and the car was fast enough to escape before someone reported us for public lewdness.

The head of his dick was pierced. Still is, as far as I know. Although I wouldn't be in much of a position to know, as I haven't seen it in years.

I've seen him lots since. Slept next to him in his bed, been analyzed by him in ways I wouldn't take from most friends, much less a stranger—regardless of whatever psych degrees they might have.

Almost irritatingly, he's always right.

During the period of our lives that we were fucking, he had special condoms with a baggy tip. When people ask if I've ever had sex with someone with a ring through their cock, and then ask what it's like, I hedge my response with the preamble that I've only had one such partner.

But.

It's like all the rolling internal stimulation of being fingered by an expert with all the entwined bodies and pelvic bone-to-clit sensation of being fucked by someone with a penis.

We were once friends with benefits. Now we're friends, without benefits, and also without the "just."

On Distraction

August 13, 2017

I just wanted to blow him, and can't recall why. Maybe I felt like having sex but didn't feel like taking my panties off, didn't want to be penetrated. Maybe it was a sudden whim for dick in my mouth.

Sometimes, it's fun to go into a sexual interaction with focus on another human. Forget my body, ignore any input that could be a distraction, inhale their balls.

Maybe this doesn't happen for you. Maybe the gender you prefer is different. Maybe you're not into oral sex.

He has this habit of prioritizing female pleasure. There's a whole flock of adult men who internalized the same values and carry the same concern about being "that guy." You know, the technical cartoon one who ejaculates, rolls over, and immediately starts snoring.

It's lovely in a lot of ways. Sometimes it backfires and they start counting orgasms. Overall, though, better a sexual partner care to the point of nervousness than not care at all.

But back to that blowjob. I wanted to focus on it. He wanted to run his fingers over my labia. I grabbed his wrists, gently planted them next to his hips, and watched as he immediately rolled his dominant hand out of my grip.

I thought "well, no need to broach the subject of being tied up." Instead, I said, "Not naturally submissive" and one or the other of us broached it later.

Radley, for Russ

April 23, 2017

I'm guessing you read Ashley West's tribute to Radley Metzger at the *Rialto Report*. I'd love to tell you about meeting Radley. It's sort of a saga though, so I'll start in the middle.

…of this party celebrating Catherine Robbe-Grillet and Toni Bentley, where a well-groomed British man walked over and asked if I'd like to meet Radley Metzger. *The Image* was one of Radley's films, and he'd worked with Toni on a few small projects. He was still living in New York. And sitting on a couch in the next room.

After I began wondering how a person who is questioning the integrity of their reality testing might verify it, but before I'd gone too far down that rabbit hole, I said yes. A few minutes later, Ashley had volunteered to coordinate lunch.

———

We met at a diner in Midtown. Pretty shortly after we'd ordered, Radley told a story about filming in the former Yugoslavia. He'd had a crew from all over Europe, and if the day went too far into overtime, the set would become Tower of Babel-esque. (Or, you know, whichever Why We Have Many Languages myth you favor.)

Radley knew how to quickly find points of commonality and use them to develop a rapport. Trust between performer and director is integral to good work, so it serves a director well to start building it early on. His life had been so fantastical that he could dig up a personal anecdote for any occasion, and he shared those stories freely.

———

Mostly, though, we talked about arnica. It's odd, I googled "radley metzger arnica" and didn't get a single result containing all three words—but that man loved arnica.

Radley swore by it for inflammation and was quick to follow up with a reminder that inflammation is linked to stress and poor health in a sort of vicious triangle. I happened to swear by it for bruises—and abrasions when mixed in petroleum jelly.

(I'm going to go one step past "this is not medical advice" here and proceed directly to "you probably really shouldn't go rubbing mildly toxic flowers and basically K-Y into broken skin and it's a miracle I haven't developed unsettlingly neon patches or some other absurd reaction.")

He'd either made or begun a documentary on arnica, and spoke at length about his visits to the European mountains the plant grows on.

———

Radley was active and lucid through his 80s, and while I'm sad to have missed the chance to work with him, I'm happy to have participated in the fun he seemed to have thinking about it. And it may be for the best that he left before he felt like he had no more to give.

Loop

December 11, 2017

It was still there, years later. That immediate magnetic comfort. When I did pull away from our hug, I didn't pull away by much. Our faces stayed close together for long enough to wonder if they might kiss me, and, if we did kiss, if it would still feel like inhaling some kind of balmy cloud. The attraction hadn't waned at all.

I'd thought he might kiss me after the show. I had my arms wrapped around his neck. We were swaying gently, and his eyes looked so large because his face was so close to mine. He didn't.

I'd thought he might kiss me when he came into my apartment. I'd also thought he might kiss me two hours in, with my leg draped over his and my face snuggled into his neck. Finally, four hours after he'd arrived, he kissed my cheek and made a move towards my mouth. I held his head in place with both hands and met his lips with mine.

His tongue thrust into my mouth. I flattened my own tongue against the bottom of his, enjoying feeling so open. Or maybe the feeling was opened. Every muscle in my body relaxed towards him. I thought "This is the kind of kiss you dream of capturing in pornography."

He said mentioned he remembered that weekend so vividly. I said "What weekend?" and immediately regretted it. I could see in his face that he'd thought I was serious. "I'm sorry—I shouldn't have been flippant. I remember the weekend you're talking about relatively well."

————

We'd spent every possible hour together, outside of work and a wedding. We'd hooked up, had sex, lounged, talking with skin pressed against skin. He'd found it romantic, the way I was bouncing from hotel to hotel. I'd felt near-disastrously irresponsible— what gainfully employed adult can't manage to secure long-term housing quickly?

I'd written about it afterwards, around the time I started taking capitalization seriously. It was the first—but far from last—time I zoomed in on the joys of all the kinds of touching that aren't directly sexual. It was the first time I tried to pen with words that gravitational pull of ease.

Gravity

October 2, 2017

"You have a siren-like effect on me."

"Good that you've also got a self-preservation instinct."

Actually I'd had no idea. They've always got this air about them when they leave, as though they've turned their gaze to the next appointment, and are striding purposefully towards it. Instead, it turned out to be a glimpse of the discipline it takes to tear themselves away and handle necessary tasks.

The amount of time we've spent ruefully sharing feelings we'd thought were obvious is significant. Two people, both assuming the other is far less invested, trying to avoid appearing too eager.

———

The previous night, they'd referred to me as the center of gravity.

There's a mountain of comments stashed somewhere in my brain, some accusing me of behaving like the center of the universe, others going to far as to call me a goddess. This gravity metaphor felt like neither. It felt like a refreshingly appropriate way to romanticize a human, from earth.

A humanizing glorification, if you will.

———

There's a terrifying responsibility that comes with being an important part of someone's life. To disappear abruptly is to cause pain. Dissonance between speech and actions stirs up fears related to attachment.

Withholding emotions or life events says something , like a speech act does, and sometimes what is said is not what we mean. We communicate so much with our bodies, and our silences.

(And I'd rather be a fish-woman, or part of physics, than a myth or an astral feature.)

The Squee and the Chill

March 27, 2015

Early exposure to Fosse, my time performing at notorious late-night theatre/den of debauchery The Box, and that first viewing of *Café Flesh*. Maybe a dash of James Bidgood's work and process. These are the major influences that added up to make *Graphic Depictions*.

I've now seen *Café Flesh* too many times to count. Paul Fishbein (one of the founders and former owners of AVN) asked me to talk about it for his Showtime documentary *X-Rated: The Greatest Adult Movies of All-Time*, on the history of adult films and my god, did I babble.

And then, one day, I had a reason to try and get in touch with Rinse Dream, director of *Café Flesh*, and quite possibly the most difficult former pornographer to track down. Eventually, with the help of a couple of other former pornographers, Mr. Dream's email address was acquired.

I actually squealed, out loud. The cats flattened themselves to the floor and stared at me with huge eyes. Half an hour later, I'd re-written the subject line approximately fifty times and started on the body of the email.

You'd think that by twenty-eight, I'd have managed to develop some chill. Or if I couldn't have chill of my own, I'd've found a synthetic substitute to keep in my pocket for when it is needed. No such luck.

(If this next story seems well-rehearsed, that's because I tell it to everyone who proclaims their own giddy nervousness when meeting me at a convention, and nine times out of ten it does seem to put them at ease.)

In 2010 Terry Gilliam was at a party. I was also at this party, and someone offered to introduce me to him. We walked over and the person making the introduction said "Terry, this is Stoya. She's a big fan of your work. Stoya, this is Terry." And then I said "ohmygodYou'reSoCool(gasp for air)CanITouchYou?"

Exactly like that. All the words smushed together.

Terry—who is the only person who can say what was going through his head at the time—replied "Sure." So I slowly reached out with one of my index fingers, poked him somewhere in the vicinity of his bicep, and squealed.

The person who'd introduced us apologized to him profusely while gently pulling me away.

Earlier this year I was in a sketch for The Daily Show. They were filming in Vegas. When I checked into the Bellagio, the desk clerk asked if we could talk about the email address the room had been booked with. I didn't want to talk about the email address because the address belonged to someone from *The Daily Show*, and telling a stranger what I was in town for felt like it might jinx it.

I did tell the desk clerk, and it didn't jinx it.

I woke up the next morning and put on my professional face—metaphorically, but also physically because there is, after all, a certain look which reads on camera as "porn star" and that look requires a certain amount of makeup.

I made it through all of the hellos and the whole day of shooting. On my way out, the producer thanked me for being a part of the show.

That's when I SQUEEd. All caps, high pitched. Then words rushed into each other (as tends to happen when one is extremely excited and has no chill.) Absolute paragraphs of OMG fell out of my mouth. I'm pretty sure I actually said I ought to retire immediately, because I doubted any cooler gig was in the cards for my career.

There's no point to this piece other than the fact that while some of us have chill, some of us really, really don't.

Graphic Depictions, Scene 03

April 30, 2015

Christian has one of the sweetest dispositions in adult entertainment, and a beautiful Texan drawl. Dana Vespoli is a stone fox and a stone-cold pervert. I adore them both, all the more for their help in bringing a longtime fantasy of mine to life.

For years I've been trying to find a reason to make a rhinestoned banana phallus that ejaculates whipped cream. I have no clue how the image got into my head, or why it showed up every time I was asked to come up with concepts for a stage show or photo shoot.

But it did. And when someone asked for specifics about what *Graphic Depictions* would involve, that sparkly, yellow, dairy-product-shooting cock was right there, blocking the rest of my vision.

So I tried to make it a reality. I acquired dildos that ejaculate and could be strapped on. I found out the hard way that silicone is a major ingredient in most of the secret blends used to make lifelike dongs. I also found out that silicone is one of the few substances e-6000 glue can't stick a rhinestone to.

I went back to the drawing board. Literally. I tried gold leaf, researched materials and glue, thought about molding a phallus myself.

I found a maker of glass dildos and inquired about the possibility of having a hollow one made. They said no, since hollow glass can shatter inside an orifice. I explained that the abrasive quality of rhinestones—an inherent part of what gives them their sparkle—would preclude insertion regardless. Swore

up and down it would not actually enter a hole on anyone's body.

They agreed to make my banana cock. I sent over the names of the specific colors to use, tried my best to explain the stone placement method I use to achieve maximum sparkle, and worked on how I would install the squirting mechanism once my phallus arrived.

When it arrived, two days before the shoot, it looked like a pineapple.

Bananas and pineapples are both fruit. Both have a decent amount of vitamin C, though pineapples have more. However, only one has lots of mildly radioactive potassium. Only one is associated with cream closely enough for the whipped variety to seem even remotely logical bursting out of it. And only one has a history of suggesting fellatio when eaten whole.

Turns out, there'd been a communication error between the glassblowers and I.

An impromptu performance of temperamental artist hysteria ensued; foot stamping, tears, declarations of postponing the project, the whole nine yards.

And then someone asked if a regular banana would be ok. At that point, as long as a male-bodied person put it in their mouth, a regular banana was totally okay.

Graphic Depictions Episode 03: A woman with huge tits and a banana. A man who loves every inch.

Cocks

April 15, 2015

I was having drinks with a friend during the early stages of winter. They invited another friend, a small-framed woman, to join us at the bar. After she arrived, after glasses of whiskey and shots of whiskey and still more glasses of whiskey, she said something about having a dick.

I don't remember if it was about wanting to have a dick, or curiosity about what it would be like to have a dick, or happiness that she did not have one. I'd had a lot of whiskey, and I was distracted by her shell-pink lips.

I do remember exclaiming "Dick for a Day!"

Dick for a Day is the name of an anthology published in 1997. Fiona Giles asked a number of women to write about what they would do if they had a cock for 24 hours. Some of the pieces are brief opt-outs: the writers would stay in bed and try to sleep until it went away, or their behavior wouldn't change. Others are a window into a very binary kind of feminism. Many are more about the power and respect assumed to accompany a penis, than about the actual cock.

I tracked down a used copy, had it sent to my apartment, and passed it to that woman with the beautiful mouth through our mutual friend.

Less than eight weeks later, Kayden Kross picked me up from the Los Angeles airport. Over dinner, we discussed the last bits of pre-production for *Screwing Wall Street*, and then we headed off to The Pleasure Chest to purchase me a cock of my own.

See, the freshly minted "Wall Street Porn Star" wanted toys in her scenes with other women.

So, Kayden bought me a cock. And a harness. The last time I'd tried to fuck someone with a strap on was in 2007. The hardware has gotten a lot better, in both form and function.

I felt perfectly comfortable with my ability to stand there, torso leaned slightly back to avoid blocking the light, and get my dick sucked. I was deeply unsure of how to penetrate a person's vulva without nerve endings on the parts I was putting in them and how to keep our bodies open to the camera from the phallus-having end of the situation.

But I'd been on the other end of it a number of times and I had two male performers willing to show me the ropes. For missionary and doggy, there's a twist of the hips and a bending of the dick in the opposite direction, or another option for doggy called the up-and-over—that shot frequently dominated by testicles and man-taint. This is one of the reasons longer penises are considered an asset for male performers.

As I said goodbye to someone leaving set, I went to hug them as I would normally do. They didn't want my hug that day because they didn't want to be poked by the rigid phallus protruding from my crotch.

We started shooting the sex scene. After the blowjob, I bent Veronica over a desk chair and positioned the head of my cock at the opening of her vulva, gently pushing in. I heard an "ow."

I froze and waited for her to move away at her own speed. Asked if she wanted to scrap the strap on or do most of the active fucking herself. We tried again, there was another "ow," and then my dick went out the window—or, actually, into a garbage bag, because re-using penetrative toys is generally frowned upon for sanitary reasons.

We scissored instead, and it was less awkward than having a penis. Which really says something.

Cocks: You can keep them.

Trigger Warning: My Inbox

December 25, 2017

The week of 18 December 2017 was a rough week. Some people assumed Serbia was the issue, so I now feel a need to explain myself further:

The issue is the US. The issue is the conversations about boundaries, consent, and violation that are happening in the US, and the way that Western men react to these subjects—perhaps not all men, but literally every Western man I've spoken to for more than three minutes this month.

The issue is also the way that women in the US media email me about these subjects, asking for commentary—like I haven't publicly stated that I will move on with my life, and will simply retire if the media refuses to allow that to happen while I remain in the public eye.

I am fortunate to be in a place where I don't need Ritalin to do my work at the level expected of me. I am fortunate to be in a place that helps me feel stable, where many of my friends are available last minute for a coffee or dinner and we can share our issues as opposed to steam-rolling each other with them. I am fortunate to be in a place where I am able to have my feelings as they happen, process them, and write about them if they're organized enough. I am fortunate to be in a place where I am treated as a human above all else.

If I had been in New York last week, I'd still be in a funk. I'd be exhibiting physical symptoms of depression and hypervigilance. I'd most likely be experiencing a domino-like cascade of flashbacks.

But I'm not in New York. I'm in Belgrade. Where my only insecurity stems from the fear that I won't be allowed to stay here. Where I can move freely through the city, where no one has ever interrupted my dinner to demand a photo, where no strange man has ever put their hands on me inappropriately.

God save me from men whose default mode is to make assumptions, please. God save me from feminists who forget that I am human, too.

boop

May 1, 2017

A long, long time ago, in an Internet that was… um… this exact one, there was a troll.

They seemed to keep to Instagram, and devotedly told me whether they had been able or unable to fap to each of my posts. It was impossible to figure out what would be fapped to and what would be unfappable.

(Fuck, I'm having way too much fun conjugating *fap*.)

One day, a journalist asked me about trolls. Generally, when journalists ask about trolls, it seems like they want to hear about the horror show in a way that feels uncomfortably close to that voiceless-pornstar trope that just refuses to die—the "sex worker as unable to speak for themselves" meme is more viral than cold sores.

(In case you're uncertain: We aren't voiceless. Some of the world just acts earless when we're talking.)

So instead of the horror show, I told the journalist about the "fapped to this/no fap" comments. Specifically, how hilarious I found it. I remember saying "What if they find out I enjoy it and that ruins the fun for them and they stop?"

Shortly after, they disappeared.

(This would be a great place for the sad trombone sound.)

I bemoaned this to my friend Chris Steffen, and he started leaving *boop*, *no boop*, and *can't boop*—as applicable—on my posts. It makes me giggle every time.

Monopoly
August 1, 2017

Before I installed a sufficient buffer in between myself and the comments section, I noticed some trends in commentary. The most topical being that my smiles and laughter during sex scenes resonate with some people as "not how real women have sex" or just "fake."

The paradox is—I tend to be even more giggly off camera. A and I are particularly boisterous together. Learning the knack of spanking seems to be only as high a priority for him as blowing a solid raspberry.

(I'm into it, in case that wasn't clear.)

Last night though, mid-finger stroke across my clitoris, A mentioned Uber.

Immediately my mind jumped to some discussion of Jon Ronson's audio-only piece on Manwin (currently operating under the name MindGeek), piracy, and independent pornography. My vulva went "NOOOOO, we're having fun" while my brain went "80% of pornography is viewed through them. MONOPOLY."

And, you know, monopolies aren't particularly sexy to me. He quipped about only name-dropping Lyft or Juno from now on when we're in a bed, and the laugh was as good for me as the orgasm that followed.

Hot [Redacted]

March 30, 2015

That's his identifier in my phone. Hot, [Redacted]. Fantastic to fuck with.

He's got those beautiful torso muscles that happen on people who live life with their whole bodies. A coherency of flesh that just isn't replicated by targeting muscle groups at a gym.

When I told him he should take my phone number, that he should pick a day and arrange some casual but date-like reason to meet, I thought we'd be all physical.

But he's two for two with book recommendations. The first aspect I find appealing about this is the fact that he reads. The second aspect is that he recommends books I haven't read yet, and so far do like.

This loaned copy of the second book, *The Dispossessed*, has underlined parts, giving me a snapshot of his mind however many years ago when he first took a pen to it. I like this mind.

He said his bookshelves were all political theory and sci-fi. I said they were the same. I also see the second half of Sid Meier's career as wonderful propaganda, though, so clearly I've got some opinions about speculative entertainment.

The two cats I live with are less likely to complain about noise than Hot [Redacted]'s two roommates. Most of the time when we're together, we sprawl in my bed, our limbs tangled. No pants. I refuse to choose between squeezing him with my arms, hearing what he says, and kissing his mouth.

He said something deeply romantic once, and I

responded with "swoon." He said, no, he was the one swooning. I said "Okay then, you swoon. I'll bask."

Later he wrapped one of his hands around my ass and trailed a finger across my labia as I laid across his chest. Finger fucking as an enjoyable means more than hot pursuit of end.

Don't get me wrong—the latter is great—but sometimes it's coming like a test of endurance. Unsure if the orgasm is being wrung out of my body or if my body is wringing it out of myself. Giggles afterwards because I can't believe I survived the violent implosion.

The former is slipping under the surface of a warm bath—coming as being wholly engulfed. Relaxing into the scent of him, which I can only describe as hand-sharpening a pencil in the middle of an old green forest.

I hate camping. I love the way he smells.

Another day, I'd woken up on a friend's couch in a bunny costume with dirty feet from walking barefoot in the city (I know, it's a terrible habit, but I've had all my shots.) Hot [Redacted] picked me up, took me home, and brought me pizza while I lounged in the bathtub.

He looked at me, with mascara smeared around my eyes and greasy cheese on my chin, and deemed me perfect in that moment.

I looked at him, standing in the doorway, and I fell. Hard.

Graphic Depictions, Scene 05

August 25, 2015

Ana Foxxx is untamable.

Ana's face is gorgeous and her ass is glorious. She knows both of these facts but she still responds to compliments with a pretty smile. Her submission to Ramon and Toni Ribas is freely given yet remains hers to retract at will.

As the three performers were getting dressed for their scene, I heard them going over preferences and limits with regards to the sexual acts they would perform. I heard Ana say she wanted her partners to be rough.

There's blurry line between erring on the side of caution and respecting a performer's agency and ability to state their own desires.

"Rough" is a broad and highly subjective word, especially when bullwhips are involved.

If you tell a performer you are about to work with that you're really into rough sex without qualifying it or describing what you mean, your definition of rough and theirs have a good chance of not matching up.

Most experienced performers will proceed with caution, but if you tell them multiple times to hit you in the face as hard as they can (harder, no, HARDER) they're eventually going to hit you. In the face. Hard. Just like you've asked for.

Sometimes this ends in tears. It's usually uncomfortable for everyone, can be traumatic for the performer on the receiving end, and is also sometimes disturbing for the performer who is in the role of the top.

Best, then, to strive for specificity when discussing sexual acts. So I asked Ana to define rough.

Ana's definition of rough was much rougher than any acts we were shooting that day. Still, better to have asked for elaboration than to risk someone going too far.

I was already aware that Toni had worked at live sex shows in Europe when he first started performing, and was pleasantly surprised to find out that Ramon had as well.

This meant that they knew exactly what I was after with the project: a static establishing frame mimicking archival footage of stage productions, all the action taken with an intensity that would play for the back of the room—not just the "front row" of the closeups that would be cut into the main wide shot.

We shot the intro: Ramon and Toni walking out from side-stage and cracking their whips, followed by Ana strolling into the frame and perching on the podium. We did a second take for safety and proceeded directly into the sex scene.

I watched on the monitor as a perfect scene unfolded. Almost as perfect as Ana's beautiful face.

Around the World: Amsterdam

July 9, 2015

The center of Amsterdam's tourist area is beautifully tacky. Stores hawk sexy spandex versions of every costume a person could possibly want. I bought a condom with a blue mushroom shaped like a teapot on it. It was marked with a warning: not for insertion.

About a month before this video was shot, the women who work in the red light district were protesting the continued closing of their windows. One of the signs said "Don't Save Us, Save Our Windows." According to Felicia Anna—a window worker who maintains Behind the Red Light District in both English and Dutch—the windows are a Dutch sex worker's best option for self-employment.

I found a window that would allow me to film and rented it for a few minutes. Apparently, I take a delight in running around places dedicated to sex in my underwear, and it's all the more thrilling if the place in question might become extinct.

Then, I took Mickey Mod back to my hotel room and we had sex together. I learned how difficult it is to operate a camera while receiving oral sex. I wrote him a check afterwards, from the Stoya Inc. business account, to pay him for his performance and the release of rights so I could sell the scene.

I put my clothes back on and wandered out in search of food.

Every time I got lost, the narrow cobblestone streets returned me to the Oudekerksplein, similarly to how Las Vegas's wide corridors always spit me out in the casino.

Every time I found myself back on the Oude-kerksplein I saw the statue of Belle—dedicated to sex workers all over the world—and the Prostitution Information Centre, which was opened in 1994 by retired sex worker Mariska Majoor.

Every time, I was awed by how organized and political the women working in Amsterdam seem.

The PIC wasn't open during my stay, but I did touch my fingertips to the door and think, "Fuck yeah, self-employment."

Paris, 3rd Arrondissement

October 15, 2015

Wolf and I walked from the first arrondissement up to Pigalle in the 18th, stood outside the Moulin Rouge (a landmark in the history of sexualized spectacle), then looked for an hourly hotel.

No such luck. Sex stores full of lingerie made from raschel lace, cheap sex toys, and discount DVDs abounded. Maybe they kept the good stuff in the back? They definitely weren't handing out recommendations for no-tell motels. Whether that was due to lack of nearby existence, or my crappy French accent and syntax, is debatable.

For two long-term adult performers, the district was a bit of a yawn during the day. Yeah, sure, it used to be home to Toulouse-Lautrec, Picasso, and Van Gogh, and it was named after a sculptor. But they're all gone now. And we needed somewhere visually interesting to fuck in, for the camera.

On a hunch, we headed down to Boulevard de Sebastopol. I'd stayed near there earlier in the year and, every morning, I'd walked past older women in red lipstick, giant hats, and delightful lingerie covered by long furs. No sartorial cue signifies a sex work zone quite like people outdoors in underpants and fur coats.

Sure enough, the maps app on my phone turned up an hourly place a few blocks away. I narrowed down the choice of available rooms to three, focusing on what didn't look like spaces I already had footage of, and let Wolf take his pick. He went with the Suite Infernale.

It turned out to be a mix between a mass market paperback cover for Dante's *Inferno* and the most death metal Hot Topic has ever been. But it worked with my black lace halter bra and thong, and his leather jock strap. And it had mirrors on the ceiling.

It also had a window with a blind which could be raised. Not a window to the outdoors, a window to the next room. If there'd been people in that room they could have also raised their blind, resulting in a fairly risk-free act of exhibitionism on both parts—all the fantasy, none of the risk of interaction.

We closed the blind, though, because we were there to make porn and nobody (specifically me) wanted to deal with the potential issue of tracking them down later to obtain releases and age verification documentation, much less them spotting the camera and reporting us to management. What with all the posted signs in the lobby and elevator, prohibiting commercial sex of any kind.

And then, Wolf and I had sex. In an establishment built for interludes of fucking, in a neighborhood with sex workers leaning out of doorways, in Paris.

It was fun. I was definitely feeling my new status as a pornographer for the first time. There's something very different about performing in porn—being a vessel or canvas for the vision of another—and shooting, directing, producing it oneself. My new set of roles felt more stressful, but also more fulfilling—and more lecherous.

And I loved it.

Krk, Haludovo Palace Hotel (ruin porn?)

September 15, 2016

Zak Sabbath is a friend, and sometimes we fuck.

Zak has, on occasion, performed in pornography.*

My blue text bubble: "And what are your feelings on trespassing in Croatia?"

And Zak's grey one: "Always wanted to"

*He wrote a whole book about it called We Did Porn.

The Tip

I was drinking on a friend's apartment floor with a woman named Carol Schaeffer. She was telling me she wanted to make a documentary or news spot about some place *Penthouse* had been involved with, in what was then called Yugoslavia.

I woke up the next morning with the taste of whiskey still in my mouth and a note—either in my phone or scribbled in my notebook—that read "penthouse jugoslavija??" Once I had coffee in hand, I started googling.

Capitalism and Communism

Bob Guccione, creator of *Penthouse* and producer of *Caligula*, built a resort and casino on the island of Krk in the '70s.

In the marketing copy from Penthouse Adriatic Club, it sounds almost like Guccione thought he might heal the ideological split between East and West* by bringing Western tourists to experience Yugoslavia's beautiful coast, arranging for Penthouse Pets to mingle with socialist and Eastern bloc dignitaries. He even referred to the Pets as new soldiers against the Cold War.

(He also wanted to make money.)

The grand opening was on June 15, 1972. Guccione sold the property the following year. After over a decade of successful worker self-management, it closed, becoming a refugee shelter during the violent breakup of Yugoslavia, and falling into ruin when the last refugees were gone. But, according to the Internet, the resort still stood.

(Except for parts of the ceiling, the glass that used to enclose the lobby, and significant portions of the main staircase. Oh, and all the plumbing and copper wiring that used to be in the walls.)

This place, now called the Haludovo Palace Hotel, was built by a pioneer of sexually explicit imagery. But I couldn't dig up any explicit videos from the hotel—before or after its abandonment. So I had to have sex in it. And it had to be on camera.

How could I not?

*It is important to note that Tito's Yugoslavia split from Stalin's Cominform in 1948. And that, while Winston Churchill did include Yugoslavia in the area he described as "behind the Iron Curtain" in his "Sinews of Peace" speech, it retained its independence and cannot be neatly classified as a Soviet satellite.

Beograd to Krk

Layover in Beograd. It's 5 am. There's something like a subwoofer in my lower abdomen—the rhythmic throb foreshadowing a miserable round of menstruation. Zak asks if I need anything. I think *rakija,* but I say *water*.

A propeller plane takes us from Beograd to Zagreb. We take a taxi to the bus station, and then board a bus for what I think will be a 90 minute ride. Zak reads Rebecca West's *Black Lamb and Grey Falcon,* which the author herself described as "an inventory of a country down to its last vest-button, in a form insane from any ordinary artistic or commercial point of view."

Four hours later, the bus drops us off in Malinska. I'm wearing my goth pajamas—baggy drawstring pants made of a thin black material, a dark grey tank top, my knockoff-converse sneakers. My thighs are streaked with layers of dried blood but my usual jokes about bloodbaths in my panties seem like they'd be deeply inappropriate.

(Because they would be.)

A kid walks up to say he thinks we're awesome. Not to let the locals' staring bother us. Then he makes the metal horns gesture before walking off. It's sweet.

We do stick out among the mostly German and Austrian tourists.

When we check into the Hotel Adria, the receptionist takes our passports, saying we get them back when we check out. I'm uncomfortable without my naugahyde-y government-issued identification.

Once I'm on the bed, I curl up in a tight ball around my cramps. Zak says he's going to go scout the location, which I express opposition to by mumbling words like "producer" and "responsibility." He counters with logic and sentiments of efficiency. I show him on the map where the hotel's address is, then go back to reminding myself that my uterus probably can't actually kill me.

Scouting

Zak returns with bad news. There's one small building with the right architectural style. One of the rooms is full of papers with the Haludovo letterhead. But it's tiny and there are definitely signs of someone occupying the space in an officially sanctioned capacity.

He takes me to see for myself. I'm devastated. There's a little concrete landing we *might* be able to get away with a very quiet scene on, but it could be a little concrete landing basically anywhere on the planet within 10 degrees of latitude.

The one detail that doesn't add up is the trees. Even if the entire rest of the resort had been knocked down the day after the most recent photos had been taken, there's no way a forest would've reclaimed the land so quickly. Further attempts at thinking are foiled by my body's mutiny.

Between close proximity to an amusement park, the van parked outside the building, and the electric light glowing through one of the windows, the risk is much higher than I'd anticipated. The payoff is far lower than the sweeping views across a semi-legendary urban exploration site that I'd imagined.

Zak naps while I dig back through all the ruin porn websites, looking for information on what happened to the Haludovo.

Scouting, Round Two

When Zak wakes up around 3:30 am, I'm giddy. I have a more accurate map. We go down the paved waterfront until we spot a small flight of stairs going up into a clearing. Once we're through the trees we see a small building to our right. To the left...

...is the Penthouse Palace.

It's huge. Thick beams of decorative concrete protrude into the air above our heads. Broken glass and rusted tangles of wire litter the ground. The walls are covered in graffiti, and a small doorway leads inside. The doors have not been boarded up. There are no fences.

Zak ducks in. I stage whisper about the presumably poor structural integrity of the ceilings and floors. My phone reboots for absolutely no good reason, leaving me without a flashlight. Even though I'm thinking that this is how horror movies start, I follow him through the door.

We sneak down the hallway. Except in my case "sneaking" means "tripping over every single pile of trash and emitting terrified squeals every time our own shadows move." The empty pool, tree-like support columns in the lobby, and 3-D ceiling reminding me of one of Zak's own paintings——it's all there.

We plan to return just before sunrise, which is supposed to be at 6:02.

Sunrise

A little after 5 am, I step out of the shower. As I'm toweling, off Zak tells me there's already light in the sky. I throw my wardrobe on and start tossing gear and makeup into my backpack as calmly as possible.

I send my assistant the precise location we'll be at and tell her we'll check back in within twelve hours. She says she knows who to call at the Croatian embassy, but that she also isn't worried. I am—if this goes awry, the possible outcomes are spectacularly messy.

As I'm pulling my street clothes on, Zak says my outfit looks like a Soviet swimsuit and asks if I have any other lingerie. I think it looks more like Rudy Gernreich's monokini, but am definitely wearing it, and anyways we really need to head out right-immediately-now.

The hotel receptionist scowls at us quizzically as we do our best approximation of tourists out for an early morning stroll. Once we're back in the Haludovo, we climb up to the balcony. We push record on the video camera.

An Important Message From Zak

Zak Sabbath formally apologizes for his combat boots and shorts look; he thought we were just going to do a POV blowjob.

After

Since we've come all this way, we continue exploring. We find a spot with much better light and consider re-shooting the scene. The view of the area isn't nearly as good as where we've already shot, though, and I'm more concerned with how the location looks than I am with my own appearance.

Eventually, we hear footsteps echoing up the corridor we're in. Not the heavy stride of a police officer's boots, but definitely the crunch-crunch of a large, walking creature making its way through the same mess I've been tripping over all morning.

Aside from going back the way we came—towards the sound—the only ways out involve broken windows and a three-foot drop onto uncertain ground. My heart is pounding as we scurry through the lobby and into the parking lot.

Where we find a deer. Who knew four hooves could sound so much like two feet?

Belgrade, I Love

August 27, 2017

We'd just returned to my apartment from a museum. They turned to me and asked "If you could do anything you wanted to right now, what would it be?"

I didn't even have to think about it. I would go to Belgrade and walk in a spiral.

Belgrade makes me vibrate. There's no other way to describe it. Every time I enter the place, it's akin to a religious experience. I miss it when I'm gone, flipping through my cyrillic flashcards as a poor substitute.

(Not to imply that learning another alphabet is wasted time.)

The first time I went to Belgrade I remember thinking there was a brittle sort of joy. Mine, or theirs, doesn't matter so much as the fact that the second I landed at Nikola Tesla Airport, I wanted to hug the concrete sidewalk.

The weather was cold and I kept to the new side. All I did was walk around the residential area, talk with the hotel's bartenders, and breathe the air.

Belgrade makes me feel more alive. So alive that other times in other cities feel like a disappearing dream, or some lukewarm pantomime of living.

The second time I went to Belgrade, the weather was warm, and I stayed around the corner from the former US Embassy (it was vacated after being set on fire a couple of times during a war.) I was happy to just lay on the floor in the late evening, listening to the city wind down.

Frankly, Belgrade makes me feel like I do when

I'm fucking—the sensory input of some stimuli as simple as a gentle breeze lights up the nerve endings in my skin.

I remember noticing that I was free to walk around without harassment, that catcalls and wolf whistles were (delightfully) absent. It was the same in Greece and Turkey.

During my third visit, I felt so safe, I finally was able to fall apart, which that had been a long time coming. I had responsibilities at home, but leaving as scheduled is one of my deepest regrets.

I want to know the city deeply, memorize its streets and small landmarks, be able to visualize its monuments when I close my eyes.

Beograd volim te, will you ever feel like mine?

To Roll an R

December 5, 2017

"Radno Vreme," said the sign on the front of the shop. I vaguely assumed it meant hours of working, from context.

"Vrlo rado," said my brain, which insisted on drawing a connection that isn't really there. Many words that have to do with work begin with "rad" but not all words that begin with "rad" pertain to work. A big chunk of them pertain to rejoicing.

My mother used to warn me not to take out a map on the sidewalk in any city. The concern being that I might as well shout "I'm not from here, take my wallet."

That particular issue hasn't occurred since the spread of smartphones and high data speeds, but I did one better yesterday; I pulled out a thick hardcover English/Serbian dictionary on the sidewalk to look up 'vreme.'

It means time, in case you're curious.

———

I have a list of projects I intended to think on while I'm here. I had all these plans for sitting down and carving out structures, marketing plans, feasibility projections.

Now that I'm in Belgrade, all I want to do is, well, be here. I'm sure this is complicated by the fact that I'm off my ADHD medication, due to the way the US handles controlled substances and the amount of time I'm out of the country for. Without those pills, I struggle to maintain a linear thread of thought.

Of course, without them I also have an appetite

and am better hydrated. And I lived without them for over 30 years.

———

Anyhow, I'm here, I'm happy, and my Serbian language skills are atrocious. Off to register with the Serbian workshop my friend Carol recommended I go.

Free to Move

January 28, 2017

At some point between leaving the AVN/AEE floor in Vegas on Friday evening, and arriving in Paris on Sunday morning, I connected through Moscow.

Upon landing, I went around in circles with an airport employee on the subject of where I might be able to smoke a cigarette. Eventually, they suggested outside, but immediately told me they couldn't let me outside because I didn't have a visa.

This was a reminder that with great privilege [like a US passport] comes great potential to forget [all kinds of stuff.]

———

When I landed at Charles de Gaulle I filed off the plane, got my passport stamped, and was all ready to breeze through customs before all the people who'd checked their bags started lining up. Except…

…the customs check was totally closed. This meant there was no immediate way into France proper, and no way back to flights elsewhere.

I wasn't able to understand the voice through the loudspeaker, even when it was speaking English. The man next to me, who was French, told me they weren't being informative in any language. Then he waved his hand at the milling customs officers, who were decidedly not opening up the checkpoint, and said "Anarche." I joked, "I thought y'all were all 'fraternité, liberté, egalité'?" He said "Anarche!" again, this time a sneering declaration.

A babbling monologue started up inside my head, about how it seems like anarchy's fairest shot to date was in Ursula K. Le Guin's sci-fi novel *The Dispossessed*, and there are some really interesting concepts in those schools of thought, and philosophies that prioritize individual choice might be super incredibly necessary in the world right now, and the motto of "No Gods, No Masters" seems like one both the US and France should totally be able to get behind, right? Until my body interrupted with signs of panic and my mind switched to "DON'T PANIC."

Which, of course, works about as well as "Don't think about pink elephants."

———

See, one of the worst things to do around officers who are on alert is panic. Then you might look crazy and—in my experience—looking crazy opens up a decent chance of being escorted to the little room and/or spending a significant chunk of time in a place that feels suspiciously like a cage.

What I'm saying here is that it is easy for me to get stuck in a fear-of-panicking feedback loop. Especially when a situation is mirroring earlier parts of life in which I was terrified for immediate reasons and thoroughly trapped. So I went to the bathroom and used the sink water to swallow some of my psychiatrist-prescribed anti-anxiety medication, which is less chewable than Xanax but also, supposedly, way less addictive.

shrug

Approximately half an hour later, the loudspeaker voice explained that we'd been held due to a piece of unclaimed baggage, and were now free to be processed through customs.

———

I'm aware that our movement is controlled by

uniformed officers and subject to government whims, especially during air travel. But that control isn't something I'm used to being immediately confronted with. That control isn't something most US citizens are used to being immediately confronted with during travel—yet.

Regardless, that frightening little room is something the US has been confronting people with for years, in the name of "fighting terrorism."

Where in the World is Carmen San DiStoya?

June 13, 2017

I left, for a safer-feeling place, because I felt I was under some threat of invasion. I'll explain.

A few years ago, I'd finished my shift at Exxxotica New Jersey, and was being taken to my hotel by Steve—not the roommate Steve, a different Steve. A stranger, male-presenting and much bigger than I am (both horizontally and vertically), inserted themselves into my physical path.

It'd been a long day, so instead of "excuse me, I'm no longer on the clock" he got "I WILL HARSHLY BEAT YOU with my bag of super skin ™ orifices." The other Steve let the whole interaction play out because he was perfectly capable of intervening if necessary, but knew that most likely he'd just get a good show.

The strange man mumbled about whether I was scared of him or something.

––––––––

I was in no shape to communicate this, but fuck yes, I was scared of him or at least put on a kind of alert. Life has taught my body that humans who are larger than I am are giant spike-y question marks. Like, they could be great, or they could do something physically or psychologically injurious on purpose. The only way to find out is to risk an interaction or watch if someone else decides to take that risk.

––––––––

Molly Crabapple once interviewed me live, in person at the NYC SoHo Club. A guy waited through the whole interview—during which we discussed art, sex, politics, pornography, directing, and how it felt for me to be in charge. When question time started, this guy put his hand up, and asked how I'd found being empowered like that.

I don't think I literally spat, but I was suddenly almost entirely cat. I said: It isn't the empowerment, it's the fucking entitlement. Empowered feels as though that power can be revoked according to someone else's whim. Entitled means it is far easier to believe that that power is actually mine.

He didn't get it. At least not that evening.

———

Every public appearance takes a lot of preparation and recovery for me. I go into interviews and events as open as I possibly can. For me, this is the way I must do my work in order to feel right.

If you ignore my "no" and ask again, I start to feel like someone is trying to push, so then I disappear. Understand?

How to Do Things with Objectification

September 17, 2015

(Nancy Bauer's *How to Do Things with Pornography*, reviewed for *The Smart Set*)

In *How to Do Things with Pornography*, feminist philosopher Nancy Bauer refers to a specific idea of pornography: the inherently harmful boogey creature that anti-pornography feminists have railed against since the seventies. A significant portion of the book is spent discussing the flaws in the anti-porn rhetoric of both Catharine MacKinnon and Rae Langton. All of which is in service of what seems to the true focus of the book: arguing against philosophers' interpretations of JL Austin's *How to Do Things with Words*.

Austin's philosophical work centered around language, specifically focusing on illocutions, perlocutions, and speech acts—uses of language where saying something is also doing. In the fifty-five years since Austin's death, a number of anti-pornography feminists have referenced Austin's work in their attempts to undermine the protection that the first amendment provides adult films and the people who make them by framing it as some act other than speech. Bauer disagrees with some of their finer points.

Declaring the idea of pornography as a form of speech to be overly simplistic, Bauer begins the wrap-up of chapter five with a list of questions: "Who is doing the speaking? The subjects of the photographs? (And are they subjects or objects—or both?) The pornographers? And what exactly is being said? And to whom?"

Instead of attempting to answer those questions, she expresses surprise that "none of the people on either side of the pornography debates appears to be interested in doing [this work]." Bauer concludes by suggesting that that these questions are not explored due to the amount of pornography one would need to view, and the amount of introspection one would need to have regarding that pornography and feelings on it. This would be an understandably distasteful task for people who believe pornography is inherently abusive towards women as a whole.

Defining pornography and exploring what can be done with it are not Bauer's subject. In *How to Do Things with Pornography*, pornography is merely the means with which Bauer achieves her ends.

Bauer treats pornography as a tool, using it to discuss the academic discourse surrounding porn and sexual objectification, her interpretation of Austin's lectures, the authority of philosophers to describe, and also their responsibility to consider what their own words do. This leads me to wonder if Bauer considered her own acts of objectification committed towards pornography—as a profession, category of media, and community of people who create it—throughout the course of her book.

I'm a pornographer. I have performed in a number of explicit videos, been professionally naked for more than a decade, and consumed a significant amount of all types of pornographic media. I believe that Bauer's work checks off no less than three items on the list of Martha Nussbaum's notions of objectification and Rae Langton's additions to it. Bauer lists these notions in the third chapter before arguing that Nussbaum is incorrect to frame objectification as an action that can be negative, neutral, or positive, but she does seem to accept Nussbaum's notions as a useful quantification of objectification.

Instrumentality is shown when Bauer uses pornography as a way to discuss her understanding of *How to Do Things with Words*, failing to define it or engage with it herself while using it for her own purposes in dealing with Austin.

Fungibility is shown when she hints at a description of pornography's powers to arouse, stating that "within the pornographic mies-en-scene, there is no space for the concept of objectification." Bauer effectively erases a number of pornographers who explicitly tackle the concept of objectification in their work—examples which include Rinse Dream's *Café Flesh* (1982), Kayden Kross and Manuel Ferrara's *Carter Cruise: Wide Open* (2015), and my own work, *Graphic Depictions* (2015)—and exhibits a tendency to conflate the porn she has either consumed herself or consumed others' descriptions of with all porn.

Silencing is shown in the glaring omission of any quotes from pornographers, be they producers, directors, performers, photographers, or writers. While Bauer's book does focus on philosophy, she repeatedly references the words of Catherine MacKinnon—who, while a formidable lawyer and holds a PhD in political science, is not a philosopher. Since MacKinnon's opinions are deemed authoritative enough for inclusion, failure to include or acknowledge at least some of the writings of pornographers—published in various books, academic examinations like the *Porn Studies Journal*, even mainstream publications such as the *New Statesman*, *The New York Times*, or *The Guardian*—can be understood as silencing of pornographers.

I'm sure that Bauer's comments on Austin's *How*

to Do Things with Words are a worthwhile addition to the philosophical study of illocutionary force. Unfortunately, her choice to build this critique around pornography without deeply observing or accurately describing it—or even taking into account the work of modern academics regarding pornography—leaves her book littered with factually incorrect statements and wildly inaccurate generalizations.

Surviving the Spraytanpocalypse, Part 2

February 3, 2017

We all know food is necessary to keep our bodies and minds running, correct?

Some people get hungrier when they're stressed. Others don't seem to have any appetite changes. Some tend to forget to eat, or feel unable to.

(I'm not here to entertain qualitative judgement or anything that smells remotely like body shaming. Please respect this.)

I fall into the latter category. I'm prone to getting so immersed in a project, or driven by the urgency of it, that I don't feel the hunger alarm going off. If an emergency interrupts my sandwich, I won't remember the sandwich until the cats have dragged half of it all over the kitchen. During periods of extreme stress, chewing starts to feel exhausting, and anything I do manage to chew does that gluey, feels-like-a-rock-in-my-abdomen alchemical awfulness.

This can interfere with thinking clearly, and can start to perpetuate itself--the less clearly you think the less you prioritize needs like food. But what can be done?

If you seriously can't eat a meal, drink it.

Yogurt, soup broth, Ensure, Slimfast, Orgain, Soylent, those protein shakes bodybuilders always seem to have around. Whatever you can find/afford. It isn't ideal, it isn't a sustainable lifestyle, but it is better than no food at all.

Also better than no food: a banana, three bites of an oatmeal bar—which you can totally wrap back up and shove in a pocket for three more bites later, and pretty much any ingestible substance that isn't coffee, candy, or booze.

But how do we try to prevent the situation from getting to that point?

———

Make sure to keep whatever semi-non-perishable stuff you can almost always eat stashed somewhere. Raw carrots and frozen pasta three times a day is better than drinking your meals. Or, you know, whatever your equivalent of that is.

Ask each other "what was the last meal you ate?"

(Fuck, I wish I could remember where I picked that one up from.)

See, "are you hungry?" requires that the person being asked be aware of sensations like hunger, or even have sensations of hunger. "Have you eaten?" is super easy to say yes to without realizing how long it might have been.

"What was the last meal you ate?" on the other hand, tends to get responses like "Oh fuck, one bite of a sandwich before the phone rang at like 10am and now it's past sundown." Or "Thai food a few hours ago, but the rest is in the fridge and I'll eat more of it the next time I get up from my desk."

———

And for friends who are too slammed/overwhelmed/low on funds/exhausted to acquire and/or prepare food themselves: if you've got the cash to spare, most delivery apps will allow you to send food to other people—even in a different city. All you need are their dietary restrictions, the address they're at, and their consent.

Mid-December 2015

May 18, 2016

The principal photography on *Ederlezi Rising* was complete, though the first few scenes of the movie still needed to be shot and funding for post-production was a looming question mark.

I'd been largely protected from the media shitstorm, thanks to Kayden, Joanna, and putting an away message on my email and blocking all but a few numbers in my phone shortly after arriving in Serbia. This was great while I was trying to focus on the movie, but also meant that I had no idea what I'd be walking into when I arrived home.

And, for the first time since 2009, I'd flown without Xanax. I was so proud of myself.

Steve Prue—my roommate—and Hot [Redacted] came to pick me up from the airport. Steve has a car, and during the times we're living together he picks me up any time he's in town.

It wasn't abnormal for Hot [Redacted] to ride along. Or to take the train out to meet me on his own. But it was completely abnormal for Steve to come into the airport. Steve has always been a "I'll be waiting in the cell phone parking lot, call me and I'll meet you at the passenger pick-up curb" kind of guy. I appreciate the efficiency, and I don't have to walk nearly as far that way.

This time, Steve and Hot [Redacted] were waiting at the border control exit. Which was a deviation from an expected routine. One that Steve and I had been following for years.

Someone had thought it would be a nice surprise.

Which meant that my behavior deviated from the routine of big hugs and immediate so-glad-to-see-you that Hot [Redacted] had reasonably come to expect.

It would be easy to say this is the moment that our relationship began to fall apart, but relationships have many moments of difficulty and some survive them all. We'd never used the words *boyfriend* and *girlfriend*, because I'd become superstitiously against them. Two or so months prior, we'd dropped both the structure we thought of as "dating," and the word itself, because neither were working for us. What even were we, aside from a pair of people playing games with semantics?

I don't know whether it was that night or some other night that week. Either way, Hot [Redacted] and I were on the couch. It was late. I was tired.

I said "Let's go to bed." He heard, approximately, "Let's go have sex."

I'd spent an entire month feeling like a human, like an artist, like anything but an object. It had been glorious. His reasonable assumption blurred into pent-up feelings about my years spent being subject to non-consensual objectification. Being treated like a prop on set, whether that set be adult, music video, or fashion editorial. The scale of my reaction to Hot [Redacted]'s sexual advance was akin to using a nuclear warhead to kill a mosquito.

I wanted to rest and hold onto that feeling of being a human being of inherent basic worth, with agency, with a right—not privilege—to dictate when and how I was touched, much less fucked. Never in my adult life, even before I started taking my clothes off in public, could I remember expecting to walk around in the world without being kissy-noised at or grabbed at. I know Serbia isn't perfect, and I'm aware of the atrocities committed during the many Balkan wars, by all sides. But every time I've been there, I've been able to just live, and that has felt magical.

But back to the situation, which had rapidly degenerated.

I was approximately in one corner of my sleeping space (more of an open loft than a bedroom) and he was firmly in the opposite corner. I was very precisely enunciating every single letter of every word I said with a hissing quality to my speech, punctuating my statements with a finger jabbed downward through the air. All six-foot-plus of his well exercised frame was telegraphing "small boy being scolded," his hands tucked behind his back.

I felt like my mother. The only thing I hated more than feeling like my mother was seeing in Hot [Redacted]'s body language a confirmation that I was behaving like my mother.

I'm pretty sure he went home to sleep in his own bed that night. If he didn't, he should have. If he did, it was for the best.

Surviving the Spraytanpocalypse, Part 3

February 9, 2017

Or: Whelmed and Overwhelmed and Force Majeure, Oh My!

Learning how to leave space for force majeure has been the difference between "as whelmed as I want to be" and "constantly tipping into overwhelmed."

I'm sure there's a specialist in the Latin language somewhere who could (and would be welcome to) chime in with the precise definition and the evolution of the term, but force majeure in common use tends to mean "a huge destructive event out of everyone's control that might happen and totally derail some-one's ability to keep plans or fulfill commitments in a way that the-royal-we would understand."

I mostly see the term in entertainment contracts. Probably because I actually read those, unlike most terms of service agreements.

My own personal force majeure-albatross is called a uterus and ovaries. Menstruation is so irreg-ular for me that referring to it as a cycle feels kind of absurd, and from what I understand, my periods are atypically vicious.

(If you're thinking about suggesting I try _____ or _____ or _____, seriously thank you but I can al-most guarantee I've already tried it. Since I'm only bringing my bloody angst up to use as an example, let's skip all that and proceed to my point.)

After a certain amount of post-pubescent life ex-perience, it became my responsibility to plan for the fact that my body will—with an unpredictable sort of regularity—do wacky stuff to my hormones (and therefore temperament) and sometimes make it impossible to, like, stand up.

_____

Now for the "BUT HOW?"

I know that in two calendar months it is reasonable to expect between 2 and 6 "period events" of unpredictable duration and severity, and that I can expect to lose an average of three weeks to the total of those period events.

I keep a Google calendar and a ribbon with a bunch of bits of paper pinned to it, both of which are visual representations of my schedule, and I make sure to leave three weeks worth of blank space in each set of two months. On my "good" days, I make sure to do literally every task I can, so projects and obligations are less likely to burst into metaphorical flames when I'm otherwise occupied.

(And when I say literally I mean Merriam-Webster's #1 definition, not the exaggeration one.)

_____

If you think I'm about to compare the Trump administration to an extra-awful case of PMS and cramps, you're correct.

It has been 21 days since J20 (or, inauguration day) and a truly stunning amount of horrific executive orders have come down from the White House.

Whether you conceive of how much you can handle at once as a metaphorical plate, a bucket for containing bullshit, or a piece of ribbon with a bunch of bits of paper stuck to it, it might be useful to leave extra space for what can only be predicted as continued unpredictability.

Force Majeur… plan for it.

Trigger Warning: Cats

December 22, 2017

There's this building I stayed in when *Ederlezi Rising* was being filmed. It's got a backyard, with a restaurant kitchen on the other side. A feral cat colony lives there.

Every other day or so, I would sit with the cats and feed them tuna or sardines. When the woman handling catering on set heard about what I was doing, she would save any leftover fish and send it home with me for them.

The night before I left, the big tom hopped up in my lap and started purring. It was beautiful.

So now, sometimes when I'm in Belgrade, I go through the building, into the backyard, and feed the cats. Especially if I have leftovers for them. I grew up being told it's a shame to waste. I still believe that. You might have seen one of the kittens on my Instagram feed.

It's been a rough three days. Partially because of events I'm only hearing about third or fourth hand, and partially because I'm in some kind of extended, bloodless PMS. It feels insane to be begging my body to hurry up and menstruate.

Tears started rolling out of my eyes when the owner of the language school I attend told me that the laws regarding language visas had just changed. They came faster the more he talked, and when he started doing math I couldn't contain myself anymore, apologized, and left.

I went to Sveti Petka and sobbed. Churches are one of the safer places to have emotions. Someone said Petak is named for Petka, like Vendredi in French is named for Venus, like Friday in English is named for Freya. Female gods. Protectresses of women. Someone said Petka's church has been a site women go to when they need help since before Christianity.

I need to bleed. I need to be able to feel safe. Unlike the last church I cried in, there were no tourists pointing me out to their children. It was warm, and somber, and beautiful.

Then I went to feed the cats. The older cats got up when I pulled the tuna tins out of my bag. The kittens didn't, because they're dead. These moments are the downside of caring.

Someone said Mercury is in retrograde. Someone said not to make any decisions until Sunday, when it passes. Someone else has said retrograde Mercury interferes with communication.

Maybe writing this is a mistake. There is still no blood.

Are You There God? It's Me, Stoya.

June 4, 2017

Before Wonderlust started, I had most of a day with no work scheduled in Helsinki. Mitcz sent me a couple of lists of places to see. A Finnish burlesque performer named LouLou D'Vil reminded me that walking can be fun by pointing out how walkable Helsinki is. Steve Prue (my platonic domestic partner) emphasized the Temppeliaukio Church—I'm uncertain about whether he wanted to live vicariously, or wanted me to see it for some specific reason.

So, I walked over to it. Even though the sky was intermittently pouring rain and hail. Perhaps because it was—when in Rome/when in Finland, yes?

The Temppeliaukio church is carved into rock. It's Lutheran, which is a branch of Christianity I'm unfamiliar with. The ceiling is a giant coil of copper, ringed with windows. I laid on a pew to look up.

My brain tossed up two memories: Rebecca West's descriptions of the underground worship spaces she reported as being Bogomil (bog is generally Slavic for god, and the Bogomils were a Christian sect that was considered heretical) and the boisterous fire and brimstone church my family went to when I was very young.

That church practiced a form of the laying on of hands, but the odd part is they didn't actually touch people until they'd already begun falling backwards. Whole lines of adult humans would be gently guided onto the floor as they started twitching and babbling in guttural syllables.

Whether you believe in a god or not, what sent those people keeling over was the intensity of their faith in one. Other strong themes included our bodies as temples of the lord, which should be cared for as such, and the concept of being called. If a member felt moved (by the hand of the lord) to the pulpit, then it was believed they should preach from it.

———

Back under the copper coil, I wondered what the Lutheran God would think of my work and of the fact that I had felt called to it. Since the practice of candle-lighting in Catholicism always seemed like a way of attaching a high-priority flag to a message to god, and there were candles on the wall, I lit one.

———

As a child, I thought these adults flailing on the floor were driven by the same intensity that made me into a perpetual hyperactivity machine. School looked like a process of removing intensity, therefore adults must need somewhere that they could be intense, and this speaking in tongues must be it.

A few years later, sex sounded like exactly the same situation—a place where adults were allowed to get their intensity out. However, I would not have been able to articulate this at the time.

———

Back under the copper coil, I remembered being wrist deep in Jiz Lee a few years ago. I felt as though I was touching the inside of god. My hand inside Jiz, in my memory, was touching the inside of god, my body contained in the rock was inside a representation of god.

Because whether you believe in a god or not, I believe it is important to understand how powerful beliefs and intentions can be. Those two things, with little else, can create and destroy entire worlds. They can unite people, and turn us against each other. They can make changes so incredible they might as well be magic.

Are you there, God? It's me, Stoya.

Trigger Warning: Religion, Science

January 2, 2018

You might have heard this before, but I grew up with a lot of Christianity around. It's part of the US South, it was part of my family, it was part of my childhood. These environmental factors have a way of sticking with you, shaping you one way or another.

You might have seen how, in a rough spot, I dig for the core of what god is. I think that belief in the Christian god is about as valid as belief in the 10-dimensional universe. I believe that belief itself has a way of changing the world, has a way of giving people the strength to persevere long enough to do more than stand against entropy. Of course, I also believe that the moon makes people act a bit crazier than usual.

People used to ask whether I believed in a religion, try to tell me I was an atheist if I said I wasn't sure. I was waiting to collect more life experience. I was pretty sure there was some larger spiritual vagueness, whether you want to call it a force, or an omnipotent God, or a bunch of small gods more like super-humans. For a time, I stopped dealing with religious people at all.

[I wonder if, later, some mixture of the remains of Trump's reality career and Star Wars will be dug out of time and taken as historical fact, starting a new religion in which golden televisions are worshipped and bits of circuitry are carefully eaten.]

Religions are a way of soothing the longing for some organization or sense in the world. Science soothes in the same way. Compressing the complexity of reality into a headline or a paragraph can help, too, whether you're on the writing or reading end. The life-optimization-hippies call this journaling.

For me, I can't write into the void. I have to be addressing myself to a person who once asked a question, even if it's years later and they'll likely never read what I write. Or communicating to six people who all expressed curiosity about the same topic.

The one functional substitute I've found is the Serbian Orthodox church's slava system. Unfortunately, nobody remembers who Great-Grandpa Draggy's patron saint was. You could call this a quest opportunity.

Sex Workers Town Hall

June 18, 2018

Someone in what looks like one of Francois Sagat's fractal head shirts with the sleeves cut off weaves through the crowd, their purposeful movement marking them as part of the event's organizational team. I'm at the first town hall for sex workers, held in Queens, NY with Suraj Patel, a candidate running in the Democratic primary for Congress.

I got my period last night, which means my upper body is curled over in an attempt to protect my abdomen from jostling. No amount of PMS is going to prevent me from missing this moment, from being in this room. I'm hoping my over the counter pain medication kicks in soon, though, because I'd like to be able to follow the conversation.

Partway through the opening panel—comprised of sex workers' rights activists, advocates, and community service providers—Ceyenne Doroshow reminds us to watch each other's backs, to check in with and keep track of each other. Applause breaks out, possibly the loudest so far. In a way, we're voting with our hands.

Suraj dives into the subject of harm reduction. Lorelei Lee, the beautiful blonde seated on the same couch as I am, leans forward. I suspect we all want to hear what the politician has to say. The PMS fog obscures memory and I haven't started taking notes in earnest yet, but the clapping indicates that we like what we hear.

Someone asks how Suraj wants to end the stigma around sex work and the people who do it—something he'd mentioned earlier. He says he intends to continue listening to and amplifying the voices of the community. He moves into some of the intersections at play: mass incarceration, economic hardship. Ending these problems would also lessen the potential for exploitation in sex work. He points at events like this Town Hall being a display of our power to push back, be heard — and actually listened to.

Another person asks about sex work and disability. Suraj shows humility in acknowledging how he himself neglects to include that in the conversation, and moves into a call for every citizen's basic healthcare needs to be met.

A community organizer reminds Suraj that he is the face of anti-FOSTA, whether he likes it or not. Laughter rings around the room. They ask what he's going to do for our community if he loses the election, what he's going to keep doing to fill the responsibility he's taken on—championing our rights. He jokes he'll keep fighting but will take a month off first.

He answers seriously that he'll figure out what he did wrong, engage in self care, and points out that he's in his early thirties and isn't going anywhere. He says "I'll be right here with you guys, the whole way through. That's a promise."

Lorelei stands up to tell Suraj she hopes he does continue to listen and to learn. She thoroughly describes how great the things he's doing are, and then explains that it isn't enough. Reducing the penalty for prostitution to a ticket isn't decriminalization. It isn't enough.

Lorelei says that protecting the rights of those of us who love our jobs is too flat, too headline-y. She points out that many of us who've been in sex work for a long time have worked under many different conditions, that we've loved and utterly hated our jobs at various times. She says she needs to hear that he's here for those of us who don't particularly love our jobs, or don't love them right now, even if that's complicated.

The furthest Suraj goes is to say that the argument for decriminalization is "very compelling," but also promises he will continue listening to the community as he forms an opinion. Then the event is over.

On my way out Suraj thanks me for coming. I tell him I'm quite happy with what I heard.

An activist behind me says "Only quite happy?" I respond "I want a bolder response on decrim. I understand the likely political reasons he can't give one, but I don't have the patience for this slow and steady." She tells me to tell him that. I smile and say "He knows."

Trigger Warning: Christmas

January 7, 2018

I got my period on Gregorian Christmas, thank Petka—the saint protector or small god of women.

Three days before, I woke up feeling fine, and then a bit after noon I suddenly felt scattered and jittery. I texted precisely this to a friend, so I have the time stamp. The next day, I found out there'd been an earthquake in Montenegro, of a magnitude and geographical proximity likely to have been felt by me and medium-sized mammals.

When I'm in LA, I know to look at Cal Tech's SCEDC if that rattled feeling comes on suddenly. Especially if nobody else in whatever room I'm in felt it. My internal earthquake monitor has never been incorrect. In the Balkans, I didn't think to check and wouldn't have known where to look anyway. A friend's neighbor told me about the Montenegrin quake the next day, and I was so relieved to know the cause of the previous day's random malaise that I melted towards the floor, onto my knees.

She, the neighbor, had felt it too. She said we're both sensitive, a little like cats. This feels true. Later she told me that many of her friends are Muslim. I told her the story of that one time I went to Istanbul and hundreds of Turkish men DM'd me pictures of their cats. It was a nice break from the poorly lit dick pics and the demands to "fukx me" sent by douchebags of all nations and faiths.

(I will never fukx you. I will also never fuck you. No, not even on camera. I prefer to work with professionals and to recreate with people I already know. Please, do feel free to share more cat pictures, though.)

———

Julian Christmas Eve day was spent with a few people from a semi-secret society (i.e. they don't immediately pop up on Google) that I will refer to as the BPC. We flew drones in a park. I entertained someone's baby with various animal impressions. It was the kind of day I would like to have in my life regularly.

In the evening, First, who is more like a brother at this point than any other sort of role, took me to his parents' home. His father, being an Orthodox priest, engages in fasting. Пост (post) is a bit like intermittent vegandom, without the lectures on meat being murder or the side-eye at my leather pants—which keep my ass warm and have lasted longer than three pairs of jeans combined. Пост food is also delicious when done reasonably well.

First's father was full of jokes and hilarious stories, which I could catch a word or two of as he told them. Then I'd wait for First to translate the rest. His father doesn't speak English, but he had a preternatural ability to understand what I was saying. Priests and pastors tend to be eerily perceptive, in my experience. I suspect it's because they spend so much time studying and speaking with people.

I don't know what the father was responding to, or if he was responding to any words at all, but he said that he has seen people change. This struck me—not because I doubt my own ability to change, but because I've been doubting whether I should have made more punitive choices in the past. What he said renews my hope.